JACK MA

&

ALIBABA

A BUSINESS AND LIFE BIOGRAPHY

Published by
LID Publishing Limited
The Record Hall, Studio 204,
16-16a Baldwins Gardens,
London EC1N 7RJ, UK

524 Broadway, 11th Floor, Suite 08-120,
New York, NY 10012, US

info@lidpublishing.com
www.lidpublishing.com

A member of:

www.businesspublishersroundtable.com

Published in collaboration with the China Translation & Publishing House (a member of the China Publishing Group Corporation)

 China Translation and Publishing House

© LID Publishing Limited, 2017
© China Translation and Publishing House, 2017
Reprinted in 2018

Printed in Great Britain by TJ International
ISBN: 978-1-911498-26-1

Illustration: Myriam El Jerari
Cover and page design: Caroline Li

JACK MA

&

ALIBABA

A BUSINESS AND LIFE BIOGRAPHY

BY **YAN QICHENG**

LONDON   MONTERREY
MADRID   SHANGHAI
MEXICO CITY   BOGOTA
NEW YORK   BUENOS AIRES
BARCELONA   SAN FRANCISCO

The church is a Western institution, while the market should be seen here as an Eastern concept. Jack Ma contrasts the sacred and holy nature of the church with the down-to-earth, everyday hustle and bustle of the marketplace.

*"Western governance, Eastern wisdom.
When the church and and the market are combined,
then the Great Ultimate is achieved."*

– Jack Ma[1]

CONTENTS

CHAPTER

1

FATHER AND SON

Hangzhou's West Lake is renowned worldwide for its beauty.

It was West Lake's reputation that had inspired Jones to come here. The Englishman stood at the door of his hotel, surveying the haze that enshrouded everything like clouds, or maybe smoke. The bright mirror-like surface of the lake, the verdant islets, the multicoloured lakeside pavilions, and the weeping willows on the banks were all enveloped in a layer of mist. There was no distinct colour contrast, no spectacular work of nature here, yet there was a quality to the scene that seeped into your mind and soul. It was as though the landscape had been meticulously handcrafted by some skilled artist.

A small boat appeared in the distance, seemingly no bigger than a leaf, making ripples across the lake. Wearing a conical bamboo hat and a traditional rain cape, the fisherman skimmed across the lake's surface with his bamboo pole. This majestic scene brought Jones to a sudden realization: here was the famous place of mist and rain south of the Yangtze River that Chinese people so often spoke of. With this realization, the Englishman immediately felt that his journey had not been in vain.

"Hello!" The gentle voice spoke in a British accent. It was obviously that of a child, but had a confident ring to it.

How could there possibly be another British traveller here? Jones, who had been standing under the stairway of the Golden Mountain Hotel for a long time, turned to look in the direction of the voice. An adolescent boy appeared in his line of vision. The boy was wearing a white shirt with rolled-up sleeves and black trousers. On his feet he wore a pair of plastic sandals. He was sitting on a bicycle. One of his feet was resting on the ground, while the other was still on the bicycle pedal. The boy grinned from ear to ear as he greeted Jones in English. Jones was rather surprised, for he was not used to Chinese children coming up to greet him in such a familiar and enthusiastic manner. Feeling rather moved, he waved his hand and replied in English: "Hello, sunshine boy!"

There was no sun to be seen; in fact, it was still drizzling slightly. Yet Jones felt that this boy's beaming smile had brought a ray of warmth to this damp day.

The boy had an unusually large head on top of a rather frail and short frame. However, his smile was truly moving. His eyes glistened and his teeth were white as snow. Every inch of his smiling face seemed to exude a glow.

"Do you like West Lake? I can be your guide for free! I am not a professional, but I can certainly teach you something new about this place."

The sunshine boy spoke clearly and fluently. Although he did not use the most idiomatic expressions, Jones could understand everything that he said. He smiled with delight. As a Christian, he thought it a good omen that he had met such an enthusiastic and charming young boy on his first trip to this mysterious country. He nodded in response.

The sunshine boy smiled even more brightly. He patted the back seat of his bicycle, signalling for Jones to sit there. Jones could hardly believe that he was here in the Far East, about to take a tour round Hangzhou's world-famous West Lake on the back of a bicycle. Perhaps this would give him a taste of the legendary East he had heard of.

Jones leapt nimbly onto the back of the boy's bike. The sunshine boy's face took on a resolute expression. He stooped down over the handlebars and struck off, pedalling with all his might as he rode with Jones through the delightful scenery.

The sunshine boy tried as best he could with his basic English to tell Jones about West Lake's ten famous tourist spots. But the poor lad was gasping for breath, and so Jones jumped off the bicycle and insisted that the boy sit on the back. As Jones pedalled, he listened to the boy talk. He asked about the characteristics of each famous spot, and the legendary tales associated with them.

These two unusual tourists each gained something special from the other. Jones gained a deeper understanding of the beauty of West Lake, and the way Chinese people appreciate beauty. He became infatuated with this paradise on earth. And after conversing with Jones, the young boy became more aware of English pronunciation. He asked Jones many questions, eager to become more fluent and accurate. Their conversation became deeply ingrained in Jones's memory.

———

Many years later, Jones happened to pick up a magazine and was startled to see a certain person's photograph on the cover. He searched through the fragments of his memory and gradually pieced them together. The photograph was of that sunshine boy he had met all those years ago.

The large head, glistening eyes, and bright smile were as charming as ever. All those years later, Jones could not forget that chance meeting by the West Lake, even though he had visited many famous places all over the world since then. Poring over the magazine, he caught sight of the name of the cover star: Jack Ma. When that sunshine boy had parted with him all those years ago, Jones had given him this name. And now the Chinese youth that he had once met by chance had become the cover star of the authoritative American finance magazine *Forbes*.

Not every man has had the honour of making it onto the cover of *Forbes*. What successes had brought the boy to such great heights? Jones could not help thinking of the story of Alibaba from the timeless classic *The Arabian Nights*. As soon as Alibaba spoke the words "Open sesame", innumerable treasures appeared before his eyes.

Jones looked at the magazine again. Jack Ma was already both chairman and CEO of the Chinese Alibaba group's board of directors. As he held the magazine in his large hands, the scene of their parting that day floated before his eyes.

The sun was setting in the west, and the West Lake had finally shed its veil of mist and fog. The blazing sun set aflame the jade-green waves of the lake. They were both exhausted. Another bicycle appeared in the distance. The rider called out: "Young man, that's enough now, it's time to come home for dinner."

It was a middle-aged man. He wasn't very tall, and looked very much like the young boy. Jones realized that this must be the boy's father. From the man's distinctive tone of voice he recognized the singular affection between father and son which he had observed since he had first arrived in the Far East. As expected, the boy called back: "Dad!"

In that moment, Jones had the feeling that the boy's father approved of his coming to the West Lake, and that was one of the reasons why the boy had given him the tour for free. The boy had already told Jones that his goal was to interact with foreign tourists, speak with them, and improve his English.

———

Jack Ma's father, Laifa Ma, was a famous folk entertainer and director of his folk association. Being so well connected, he took Jack Ma to the opera regularly. Jack Ma did not understand that much about Chinese opera, but was fanatical about the thrilling fight scenes between the knights in these performances.

He was far from being studious at school, but was very willing to practise martial arts. He was most proficient in wrestling. The fact that he was neither tall nor stocky did not affect his fighting abilities. As a result, aside from the many friends who followed him, he often had to carry many battle scars around with him. The most serious instance was when he had to have 13 stitches in hospital. He was a typical troublemaker at school. His mother once said that her son did not play by the rule book.

He loved to read the martial arts novels of Jin Yong. His infatuation with martial arts even impacted his actions in later life. When he established the new headquarters for Alibaba, he used many of Jin Yong's names for different areas. For instance, he called the meetings rooms "Peach Blossom Island" and "Bright Summit", while the library took the title of "Evening in the Maple Woods". These names, including "Armed Dispute on West Lake", were all inspired by that period of his childhood.

Besides his ardent love for martial arts, Jack Ma's adolescence was characterized by his love of English. His father liked to say, "I was the spade that dug up his skills. After I discovered his talents, I used them to bury the remnants of his negative traits."

The first thing his father dug up was Jack Ma's English potential, but that was by accident. In his youth, Jack Ma was certainly not lacking in rebelliousness. His father was often on the receiving end of this rebellion. Jack Ma was rather unusual in that when his father scolded him, he would reply in English. This made the disputes between father and son quite entertaining, as his father spoke in Hangzhou-accented Mandarin, while Jack Ma replied in stilted English. His father did not complain about this, because it was these disputes that revealed the boy's talent and passion for English. In the father's eyes, talent and passion were both crucial things for a child to have. As a result, whenever he had the time, Jack Ma's father would take him to the West Lake in search of foreigners.

Even though his father had a hard time understanding English, he would still encourage and do all he could to help the boy. He did his best to think of any strategies that would further develop Jack Ma's talent.

Sometimes Jack Ma would go out with his father, sometimes he would take out his shabby bike by himself, pedalling along the banks of the West Lake in pursuit of opportunities to improve his English conversational skills.

Apart from improving his English, the contact he made with foreigners also expanded his adolescent horizons. Western culture and values, and foreigners' impressions and feelings towards the rapidly developing nation of China, all made a great impact on young Jack Ma's way of thinking. Of course, no one was aware of how he felt at the time. However, when Alibaba was crowned as "a truly world-class brand" by the media, one could look back at the adolescent of West Lake who rode around on that shabby bicycle, and realize that he must have dreamed of this success even then.

————

One stuffy Hangzhou night, the light of the full moon was reflected in the beads of sweat on Jack Ma's father's forehead. The flame in the lamp had reduced to the size of a pea. He was cooling himself with a palm-leaf fan, his gaze set on the young boy. Jack Ma was seated on one corner of the bed, silent. He had just failed to obtain a job as a security guard.

"Young Jack Ma, you must be feeling depressed right now, but if you can't be a security guard then you're just not meant to be one. But all roads lead to Rome. I've already contacted several magazine publishers. You'll start delivering magazines for them tomorrow; how's that?"

"Really?" Jack Ma's eyes lit up.

"I won't lie to you: it will be difficult. You will have to cover several kilometres on your tricycle every day. You need to make up your mind now. If you're scared of hard work, then it's better for you to decide not to take the job sooner rather than later." His father stood up.

Jack Ma also stood up. He extended an arm towards his father and said: "I'm not afraid. I'm young, I'm not afraid of hard work. Isn't it just riding a tricycle? That's one more wheel than an ordinary bicycle. When I used to ride my bicycle around, I covered several kilometres a day."

"Excellent. I will take you to report for duty tomorrow." Jack Ma's father patted him on the shoulder by way of encouragement.

The next day, the boy of the West Lake became a young man on his tricycle. He had grown taller by now. The tricycle was not new. There were countless marks on the tyres, the frame was covered in rust stains, and the saddle was cracked. As he pedalled, a strange sound would come from the tricycle. Jack Ma knew that old tricycles were no different from old people: they both struggled with heavy loads. Moreover, the back of this tricycle was piled high with books. Books are never light to carry, let alone when you have a whole pile of them.

Jack Ma's father had found this job through his personal contacts. The young man had to take the tricycle, piled high with magazines, around Hangzhou and deliver to all the booksellers and vendors. Hangzhou summers were hot. The sun beat down on the tarmac of the roads, turning them softer than sponge. There was no breeze. The weeping willows along the side of West Lake were motionless. There was only the incessant and infuriating chirping of the cicadas to be heard. Jack Ma pushed down on the pedals of his tricycle and sped off into the surging traffic under the scorching sun.

When Jack Ma's father saw his son return day after day, his little sleeveless shirt drenched in sweat, he could hardly bear to look at him. Jack Ma's exhaustion showed on his large face. The skin on his shoulders was cracked and burnt by the sun. Faced with such a spectacle, Jack Ma's father was often overcome with emotion.

"How did you get on, Jack Ma?" his father asked. "Alright, not bad," Jack Ma replied. Hearing this, his father did not know what to say. Evening fell. Jack's father sat by his bedside, rubbing his shoulders as he said to him: "It's so exhausting for you to ride dozens of kilometres a day. How come you are not able to put the same amount of effort into applying for university? Would it really be harder than all the kilometres you have to cover now on your tricycle?"

The father spoke softly, but his words sounded deafening to Jack Ma. In the middle of the night, when all was quiet, Jack Ma tossed and turned in his bed, unable to sleep. What his father had said was true! Wasn't it only his maths that needed improving? Why was it that other students did well in the examinations but he did not?

The next day, he gathered together all the maths teaching materials and textbooks he had. Every evening he pored over the difficult equations as though his life depended on it. His father was delighted. He waved away the other members of the family, signalling them not to disturb the young man.

Jack Ma spent that year riding his tricycle during the day and studying at night. However, his inherent weakness in maths could not be solved by last-minute cramming. As a result, he scored only 19 marks on the maths paper of the university entrance exam. Even when the marks for all his subjects were added together, he was still 140 marks short of the minimum required to be accepted for an undergraduate course. This unobtainable figure and Jack's dismal results dashed his family's dreams to pieces. After that, no one encouraged him to take the examination again. Yet Jack Ma himself remained resolute and threw everything he had into preparing for the next round of university entrance exams.

His family were not supportive when he failed the examination for the second time. The only person who backed him was his father, who handed in Jack's resignation letter for the magazine delivery job on his behalf and even hired a first-rate maths tutor for him.

The maths tutor's reputation was well deserved, and Jack Ma had lessons with him twice a week. The tutor's witty way of talking and humorous gestures greatly increased Jack's interest in maths – and, for any student, taking an interest in the subject is more important than anything. Algebraic formulae, which Jack Ma had once found tiresome, now took on new meaning and he began to devour equations ravenously.

By stuffing himself in this manner he was able to improve his maths ability no end, while his English remained ahead of the crowd as always.

That year, he entered Hangzhou's university entrance examination hall once again. His father came with him and stood outside, saying nothing. The July sun beat down on his face and the silver hairs on his temples glinted in the light. He waved resolutely at Jack Ma as the young man proceeded directly into the classroom without looking back. Jack Ma dumped his satchel on the floor and took a seat at the desk with his name on it.

This would have been about 1984. Located south of the Yangtze River, Hangzhou was a place filled with grace and elegance that made one feel utterly carefree. The streets were lined with places selling popular snacks that were famous throughout China. There were beautiful sights to be seen everywhere and the pace of life here was neither rushed nor lazy. Pedestrians on the street seemed to stroll along casually, as though people from Hangzhou were born with an inner calm. Perhaps it was the idyllic surroundings that lulled them into a state of tranquillity, never angry or startled.

Hence, when Jack Ma received his results, he appeared to skim over the document casually before putting it down on the table. It was his father who was rather more anxious, saying: "So? What did you get in maths?"

This was a turning point in Jack Ma's life. At the very least, it was a turning point in the course of his applying for university. Those who were successful in the exam would get into university without a hitch. Those who failed, however, had no hope whatsoever. It was extremely rare to come across anyone who took the examination three years in a row, but Jack Ma was one of them – and it was all because of maths!

"Seventy-nine!" Jack Ma played down his accomplishment, as if it was completely to be expected and nothing to make a fuss about.

As it turned out, all the work he had put in had paid off. The year he had spent studying had not been in vain, and his tutor was truly an expert. The time and effort invested by both student and teacher had been worthwhile in the end. Only two years had passed between his results of 19 and 79, but they brought about entirely different outcomes. The improvement in his maths score meant that his overall mark was only five short of the minimum to get into university.

However, anyone who has taken the university entrance examination will know that five marks can make all the difference. For many students, five marks can be enough to stop them reaching the peak of the mountain they have so arduously climbed and miss out on the opportunity to better their life chances.

That being said, luck is also a necessary part of fate. It just so happened that Hangzhou Normal University had not filled its undergraduate quota for that year and decided to decrease the minimum score by five marks.

And so young Jack Ma was accepted as an undergraduate of Hangzhou Normal University. He made no secret of the fact that in August of that year he was entering the university's ivory towers to become a favoured member of society.

As Laifa Ma watched the figure of his son leaving for university, a sense of relief washed over him. All those years of blood, sweat and tears he had spent digging away to uncover his son's talents had not been in vain. Today, he had finally seen his son leave the nest. That night, he did not sleep a wink.

Of course, this moment was vitally important for Jack Ma as well. By leaving the nest and getting into his dream university, he had greatly increased his self-confidence. He had discovered that there is nothing insurmountable in this world. It had taken so much effort for Jack Ma to get from 19 to 79 marks in maths, but looking back now it seemed to have passed by in a flash.

The key to his success was never giving up. Many years later, when Jack Ma's career had already reached great heights, he wrote the following words on his blog in memory of his father: "I was only 12 years old at that point, and yet my life was something like the legendary tale of 'open sesame' in *The Book of One Thousand and One Nights*. So many earth-shattering changes took place. However, I never felt any sense of disbelief because my father had already spent many years with his spade, searching for the precious truth of success. What he found was that you must find what interests you. You must pursue your interests and turn them into your talents. Ultimately, your talents will play the most important role in your success."

———

In his third year at Hangzhou Normal University, he was finally elected president of the student union. Not long passed before he became the president of Hangzhou's student federation.

Ever since childhood, Jack Ma had been the kind of person who would always fight for justice. It was precisely because he was willing to help others, and because of his chivalrous nature, that he enjoyed good favour among all the students.

On one occasion, a student had been stripped of his right to take an examination because of a trivial mistake he had made. Jack Ma did not know this student particularly well and they had never had much contact with one another. Despite this, Jack Ma felt that this young man was not a bad student, and if he missed out on the chance to take his examinations now, it would affect him for the rest of his life. He could not stand by and do nothing: he felt imbued with a sense of duty to help out a friend in need. Taking advantage of his position as president of the student union, he went to find the heads of department and faculty.

At that point, Jack Ma was already famous in Hangzhou Normal University for being an outstanding student. His exceptional academic record, bold personality, and talent for making speeches had made him a model student leader. As a result, he was able to attract the attention of the department and faculty leaders. After looking into the matter once again, they found that what Jack Ma had to say was quite reasonable: destroying a young man's future on account of such a small matter was unworthy of a successful educational institution. The department and faculty heads revoked their decision, and the student later managed to pass the graduation exams with ease. Jack Ma forgot about this incident as soon as it had passed; but ten years later, the very same student heard news that Jack Ma was drifting about in the booming city of Shenzhen. When he found Jack Ma, he clasped his hands and said: "As soon as I heard from my old classmate that you were in Shenzhen, I rushed over here immediately. I'll sort out whatever you need."

At that time, Jack Ma was still far from success. He was extremely moved to have come across such sincere friendship in a time of hardship. Moreover, the student from all those years ago was now a manager of a subsidiary branch of a foreign enterprise in Guangzhou.

During his time at university he gained the favour of many teachers and the praise and appreciation of many of his peers. Even in the years after he graduated, he would still get an unexpected phone call from time to time: "How's it going? Is there anything you need help with? If there is, we can help you out."

Jack Ma's large circle of friends and his willingness to help others meant that he not only enjoyed the support of his peers in his role as president of the student union, but also found his reputation spread far across campus.

He was eulogized by the scholars of Hangzhou Normal University. It was largely because of his personality that he became leader of the students in Hangzhou Normal University, then of Hangzhou Students' Union, and later all university students in Hangzhou.

It is easier to move a mountain than to change a person's nature. Jack Ma could never alter the personality that ran through his veins. In later life, he would always find himself surrounded by friends wherever he went. Even if he did not have a single penny to his name, friendship would always provide him with the warmth he needed, just like a ray of sunshine. It filled him with a sense of meaning. The reason he was able to break through so many obstacles when developing his start-up ventures was that he had a strong group of people behind him to offer him unconditional friendship.

Life is never predictable, and whenever we reflect back on what happened yesterday, there will always be something to regret. Yet who is able to predict what they should do today in preparation for tomorrow? At this early stage in his career, Jack Ma had already started to show his ability at formulating these kinds of insights.

University is always a comparatively free place compared to the rest of society. Here, students' minds are stimulated by the accumulation and extension of knowledge. There were many student-organized events. If Jack Ma happened to attend any of them, he was certain to be the centre of attention. The other students loved and respected Jack Ma for his integrity. He was a lively speaker, too: as soon as he started speaking, the other students would fall silent, captivated by his words. He was innovative in his outlook. He spoke quickly but clearly, in insightful language, and frequently offered alternative viewpoints on matters.

———

On one occasion when giving a speech, Jack Ma inadvertently swept his eyes over the dark mass of the audience. Suddenly, he met with a pair of bright, dark eyes. The glistening pupils were like a pair of black gems and were filled with sincerity, two sparks of hope. If eyes are windows to the soul, then in that instant Jack Ma looked through the windows and right into the core. He felt a reaction, an electric current, a kind of shapeless surge. It was as if two random clouds in the sky carrying electric current had collided and sent a bolt of lightning down to the ground. How this event would impact the fate of these two clouds, only time could tell.

Jack Ma was not a hesitant kind of person. He seems to have been born with a decisive personality. After the speech, he sought out those bright, dark eyes without delay.

"Hello, I'm Jack Ma. I hope that this is just the beginning of our time knowing each other. I hope that you will have time to meet with me again." He held out his hand as he spoke, a bright, sunny smile on his face.

A hesitant hand was extended slowly towards him, and Jack Ma grasped it firmly. They were both struck with inspiration. They stood looking into each other's eyes, sparks flying. "It's nice to meet you. I hope to have the opportunity to get to know you." The speaker was Zhang Ying, a calm and introverted girl who did not talk much, but was supremely intelligent. They quickly got to know one another and progressed from being fellow students to falling in love, and from there to being husband and wife.

They were just like any ordinary sweet couple, and yet there was something very distinctive about them at the same time. Zhang Ying once said: "Jack Ma isn't a particularly handsome guy. Yet I was drawn to him because he can do certain things that handsome men are not capable of, such as setting up the first 'English Corner' in Hangzhou, working part-time as a guide for foreign tourists to earn foreign currency, taking on all kinds of part-time jobs, at the same time as being one of the most outstanding young professionals of Hangzhou."

One of China's most beautiful sayings is "A husband and wife are like a pair of birds flying wingtip to wingtip." Zhang Ying was not only Jack Ma's lover and wife, but also his entrepreneurial cofounder and life accomplice. She would stand by his side, no matter whether Jack Ma met with failure or success. Whenever Jack Ma needed her, she was willing to sacrifice fame and glory in order to return home to him.

For some men, their career is everything and marriage is only half as important in their eyes. Jack Ma was lucky, for he had both a successful career and a happy marriage, each of which was mutually beneficial to the other. Not only did Jack Ma's time at university bring him knowledge and confidence, but in Zhang Ying he also gained a wise and reliable partner.

When Jack Ma left Hangzhou Normal University, his high-spirited and resolute eyes were brimming with hope for the future. Of course, there was no way he could have predicted the success he would obtain over the next years, but he believed that even though today and tomorrow might be full of cruelty, the day after that would be worth waiting for.

CHAPTER

RAISING THE FLAG

After finishing his undergraduate degree, Jack Ma went on to become a professor at an electrical engineering college. Most people would need a certain amount of time to adjust from being a student to becoming a teacher, but not Jack Ma. To him, teaching felt so natural that he could do it blindfolded. Eloquence was something he certainly had plenty of. There is no one else that the phrase "the gift of the gab" is more suited to. Many years later, one of his former students recalled: "Jack Ma was always brimming with enthusiasm when he spoke. He never prepared, but always managed to speak words of great wisdom, so his classes were very interesting. He greatly increased our interest in learning English."

As long as Jack Ma had a stage to stand on, he would have an endless amount of things to say. Moreover, he spoke fluent and pleasant English. He took to his new job, as an English professor at the Hangzhou Institute of Electrical Engineering, like a fish to water. Whenever he walked into a classroom, the students always sat in silence waiting for him. Every student wanted to listen to this short professor speaking, and his lessons were always full. Whenever Jack Ma saw the sea of sparkling eyes looking up at him, he was overwhelmed by a wave of emotion rising from the pit of his stomach. His viewpoint was always original, the pace of his lectures upbeat, and his voice pleasing to the ear. He had a knack of explaining complicated concepts in simple language. All that could be heard in the classroom was the sound of his well-modulated voice, while the students sat in complete silence. In front of a class, Jack Ma's charm was put on full display.

The Institute of Electrical Engineering was located in the nearby suburb of Xiasha. It was a large and impressive campus but, being only a science and engineering institute, it lacked qualified teachers for up-and-coming subjects such as business, trade and foreign languages – despite having a number of exceptional professors in the fields of electronics, automation and engineering. As a consequence, a talented professor of English like Jack Ma had plenty of scope for career development. Furthermore, the institute allowed him to join an international business course because of his exceptional English skills. He was therefore able to study international business part-time at the same time as teaching English there. China had only just opened up to the outside world at that point, so international business was both a popular and an unpopular subject. It was popular in the sense that everyone wanted to get involved in China's economic reform, and unpopular in the sense that there were very few people at that time who understood the subject, let alone any specialists in the field.

How should one interact with foreigners? How should one do business with them? What kind of business ethics did they have? What kind of written and unwritten rules of business did they follow? Who, in a previously closed-off nation, could possibly know how to deal with the businessmen who flocked from Europe, America, and Japan? Any Chinese person who went abroad would inevitably have some dealings with them, but was there anyone who was relatively experienced in doing so? Doing business was not easy. Working alongside one another for mutual benefit, at the end of the day everyone was there to make money. What was more, focusing on moneymaking had once been considered something shameful in China, besides the fact that it is a complex subject that is hard to get the hang of.

Jack Ma was also taking part in a learning process while he taught. What he learned opened a new door for him in life. It expanded his imagination and made him consider things from a more long-term perspective.

When China opened up to the outside world, its understanding of different international customs was suddenly turned on its head. Things that had once been the cause of fear and alarm, such as having relatives in foreign countries, Hong Kong and Taiwan, became sources of pride and status symbols.

Subsequently, international relations became an increasingly popular subject to study, especially for the owners of small- to medium-scale privately run and contracted enterprises. They had to take extra classes in foreign trade. In order to meet this demand, many night schools sprang up inside Hangzhou's city walls. Jack Ma became a specially appointed teacher at one such school, where he lectured on English and international trade.

His teaching style, with impressive lectures delivered in non-stop English, ensured that his reputation spread far and wide during that period when English teaching was so desperately sought-after. As it happened, Jack Ma was not the kind of person who would stand idle at such a time. He worked at the university during the day and part-time at the night school in the evenings, setting up an informal English class or 'English corner'. Jack Ma became very popular at the beginning of this period of economic reform in Hangzhou. Some people named him Hangzhou's number one figure in English teaching.

Jack Ma's time spent as a university professor benefited him for the rest of his life. When he later became chairman of Alibaba's board of directors, he frequently gave speeches abroad. He seemed able to pluck words out of thin air whenever required; he did not even need a script, let alone do any preparation in advance.

As soon as he stepped onto the stage and saw the audience looking up at him – including that bright pair of eyes mentioned earlier – the sluice gates were opened and words poured fourth from his mouth like a rushing torrent. In Jack's own words, "Once I open my mouth I cannot close it again."

For any outstanding entrepreneur who needs to appeal to their team, it is crucial to be able to express oneself in a clear and distinct manner, as well as deliver stirring speeches.

While lecturing on English and international trade, explaining to other people the way to make money, he also learned from the process and put what he had learned into practice. At that time, the average wage in China was quite low and no one would even consider putting their money into investments. Most of the professors at the electrical engineering college still lived in state-allocated dormitories, yet Jack Ma surprisingly managed to put some money together from various sources and buy quite a large house near the campus.

Later on, it became clear that he had actually been investing. Moreover, he had made quite a considerable profit from it because the increase in real estate value caused house prices to rise rapidly. After a few years, that house was worth a fortune. With no hesitation, he sold the property at once and used the money to buy a 200-square-metre (2,000-square-foot) house on Wenhua Road next to West Lake.

West Lake was famous, both at home and abroad. What does it mean to have a 200-square-metre home on West Lake? It caused no stir at the time, but Jack Ma was preparing a headquarters for his future venture, Alibaba. Without this house, that very same company which would cause such a commotion across the globe would have had no means to establish itself. Jack Ma had made a brilliant move by buying that house when property prices were low – yet he was still a university professor, not a businessman.

Jack Ma later spoke of this real-estate investment: "If I was going to invest in property, I didn't want it to be anything fleetingly fashionable, like those places with one or two bedrooms and a living room. If I was going to make a property investment, I was going to choose somewhere larger than those popular small-scale apartments, like the places on the lakeside, which were slightly bigger than a three-bedroom house. This would enable me to always stay ahead of the trends. If the opportunity came about, I would sell my current property and buy an even better place."

Hangzhou Electrical Engineering College later became Hangzhou Dianzi University. Jack Ma became one of the best young professors at the university through his position there. Furthermore, he had a large group of friends due to his enthusiastic and helpful personality.

He could never have predicted that in later years the friends he had made here would bear many trials and hardships alongside him. They would never leave his side, later becoming the backbone and the elite of his venture as it developed. For instance, his former colleague Peng Lei became the vice-president of Alibaba. His students Zhou Yuehong, Han Min, Dai Shan, and Jiang Fang all remained loyal followers wherever he went.

They worshipped Jack Ma. They trusted Jack Ma. They admired his talent, his witty perception, his fearless bravery and unyielding spirit. They put their trust in his character and his magnanimous selflessness. He never let them down.

Many years later, Jack Ma was seated in the broadcasting room of China Central Television, speaking to a Chinese audience of millions. He said with incomparable pride: "There is no one in this world who can separate me and my team."

His confidence and pride came from his team's sense of loyalty, and their sense of loyalty came from Jack Ma's character. On account of his character, people were willing to stick by him in times of trouble. They were drawn by his reputation, willing to give up better opportunities in order to work with him. This will be discussed more later, but let us say for now that Jack Ma's personal charm was already quite obvious at the time when he was a university lecturer.

So now Jack Ma had a job, a house, and a group of friends. Of course, he also had Zhang Ying. Considering all this, Jack Ma should have been happy; most other people would be utterly content with becoming a university lecturer at such a young age. But Jack Ma was different. Perhaps he was just born with a tendency to overthink things. People close to Jack Ma would often say: "You never knew when he was going to have a new idea. What most people do not realize is that that large head of his is teeming with ideas."

At that time, privately run enterprises were already starting to take shape in Hangzhou. Many small 'made in China' products were emerging, like the bubbling undercurrents which surged up in Hangzhou's Qiantang River, signalling the arrival of the spring tide.

The first rumbles of China's oncoming arrival were already being felt on the international stage. The world was beckoning Zhejiang Province, of which Hangzhou is the capital – beckoning China's privately run enterprises. Many business owners engaging in foreign trade were still finding it difficult to deal with foreign languages. As a result, it was only natural that Hangzhou's number one English speaker, Jack Ma, found himself in popular demand.

Jack Ma was perceptive enough to sense the rising demand for English, and to see that it could be translated into a commercial opportunity. Jack Ma, who was born with an innate sense for business, was not about to let such an opportunity pass by. Naturally, the first person he broached the topic with was Zhang Ying: he had to get his wife's approval first.

Zhang Ying was a warm, kind, and wise woman. She opened her bright, dark eyes wide and stared unblinkingly at Jack Ma. Yet again, her unbelievable husband had yet another new idea. Jack Ma paced around on the spot before looking back at Zhang Ying. "How about it, what do you think?" Of course, Ying could see an unswerving determination in his eyes. She was also very aware of the fact that if he had the courage to think up an idea, he also had the courage to put it into practice. Ying kept it brief. She just nodded her head and said: "It's up to you!"

"It's not just up to me. You need to be involved too. I need your help."

"That goes without saying!"

Jack Ma then made the momentous decision to set up a translation agency. It would be a small company that could offer professional translation services and also solve problems for his friends and colleagues.

After some careful deliberation, Jack Ma chose number 27 on Hangzhou's Qingnian Road, next to the Young Men's Christian Association (YMCA), to set up the Haibo Translation Agency. The translation agency was principally staffed by retired English teachers. Jack Ma still remained a full-time professor, teaching classes during the day and taking orders and handling business at the agency during his spare time.

In this way, splitting his time between the university and Haibo, Jack Ma took his first step into the world of business.

After some preparations, in January 1994 the place next to the YMCA on Qingnian Road echoed with the sound of firecrackers. Under a cluster of flower baskets, the translation agency officially opened for business. It measured about 30 square metres (320 square feet) in area, with a simple shop front.

Jack Ma chose the name Haibo as it was a transliteration of the English word 'hope'. In Jack's own words, Haibo represented a vast ocean of hope, for in Chinese *hai* means 'ocean' and *bo* means 'vast'.

With this sea of hope behind him, Jack Ma threw himself into the world of business. Wrestling with the tide, the little translation agency set off on its voyage. There were few staff – in the beginning, only five people. Jack Ma acted as the director. There were two retired English professors, and two young workers who had been particularly impressed by him when he worked as a part-time English teacher.

The translation agency should have enjoyed rapid success, as there was huge demand for their work. However, being the first ever translation agency in Hangzhou, it did not manage to gain the approval of either society or the market. The people of Hangzhou were wary, as was the market. The translation agency did not do well: there were very few orders. At the end of the first month, they made a gross profit of just 700 yuan, not even enough to cover the rent of 2,000 yuan.

Reality can be unforgiving. With no money to begin with and no money earned, some began to sound the retreat. Those who remained behind became gradually doubtful. Jack Ma felt increasing pressure, which was hard for him to bear. Faced with such a blow, he adjusted his business tactics. He split the small space in half and rented one half out to a bookshop in order to reduce the translation agency's expenses. He also started selling fresh flowers and gifts.

It was not easy to promote small-scale products like these. Jack Ma was still working as a full-time professor. He had free time only at the weekends. Under such circumstances, the tricycle-pedalling youth of the past returned once again. Every weekend, Jack Ma would set off to Guangzhou by motorcycle, with a big hemp or woven sack on his skinny shoulders. There, he would fill up the sack with all kinds of small products, from fresh flowers to socks and underwear – everything you could possibly think of. Then he would get back on his motorbike with his sack stuffed full of easily sold merchandise and ride the 137 kilometres (85 miles) back to the market.

He donned a workman's cloth cap and jacket. Even though he wore a beaming smile on his face, no one would have guessed he was the number one English speaker in Hangzhou. In ordinary people's eyes, he was just a pedlar of wares. Crouched among the many other vendors in the marketplace, nothing made him stand out from the crowd. No one knew that one day he would be CEO of the world's largest goods-trading platform.

"Whether you are from the south, or going to the north, come and have a look! If you don't stop, I won't come back and you'll regret it later!" Jack Ma's unusual way of hawking his wares attracted many buyers. Before night fell, all the merchandise he had brought was completely sold out.

This became a tradition for Jack Ma at the weekends. It gave him the opportunity to learn a little business knowledge and to experience for himself the selling of merchandise. Sometimes his wife Zhang Ying went with him; having a wander through the market stalls was a good life experience.

The wages of the translation agency's staff were paid on a monthly basis. Jack Ma was never late with anyone's pay. At the same time, he made the most of his ability to influence people and drew on all his available client-based resources to expand his market and bring in customers. He strove for market and customer acceptance by offering a top-quality service. At that time, Jack Ma was rushed off his feet. He was even willing to sell medicine and medical equipment to hospitals in order to keep the translation agency alive. It is hard to imagine how Jack Ma found the willpower to keep going during that time.

Keeping the translation agency going was Jack's most important task. Eventually, his perseverance and sacrifices paid off. At the end of 1994, the translation agency finally broke even. In 1996, it made a profit. Today, Haibo stands as Hangzhou's largest translation agency. The original space Jack Ma rented is now a reception office and the rest of the accommodation has been significantly expanded. Jack Ma passed the agency over to his student Zhang Hong to manage in 1999. He now had a new idea, a new target.

Many years later, Jack Ma returned to Haibo Translation Agency. He stood at the doorway to his first ever business venture. The events of that former time sprung up vividly in his mind. He took a pen and wrote the following three words: "Never give up." Those three words are written on Haibo's website even today.

Some people say that Christopher Columbus never had a destination planned for his voyage: he looked only to the next stop, and it was only when he discovered a new continent and new islands that they became his stopover. He would then move on to the next place where he would find a destination. Never give up, never stop. This is what makes a man great; perhaps it will not be obvious to begin with but, if he perseveres, then it will have a transformative effect.

———

Big-bearded Bill was an American teacher employed by the mechanical engineering college. He was very entertaining to talk to, and got on very well with Jack Ma personally. They often went for a drink together and spoke freely about all topics under the sun, from ancient times to modern, from the universe right down to the ocean. They were from two different countries, but of the same character. They were both full of passion and imagination, constantly searching and keen to learn about the world.

Jack Ma liked to drink wine. Even now, Zhang Yu Wine Cellars still stock bottles especially prepared for him. But at that time he did not have such a privilege, although obtaining wine was not a problem. He would invite Bill over to his house and Zhang Ying would cook a few dishes. Jack Ma would open the wine; the rich, mellow, sweet aroma would rise to meet their nostrils and Bill's cheeks would flush red with anticipation. He and Jack Ma both believed that wine was the best drink on earth. Bill's big nose would twitch. He would give a thumbs-up and say, "Mr Ma, excellent. Your wine is simply excellent, and your wife even more so."

Perhaps it was because he was from a different culture that he spoke so directly and to the point. Jack's face creased into a smile. He tugged at Zhang Ying who was sitting to one side of them.

At that time, Jack Ma was not only a professional university lecturer but also a specially appointed English teacher at many night schools, the translator for a number of companies, and the manager of Haibo Translation Agency. He was constantly offered work with no respite, causing his income to slowly climb higher and higher. To tell the truth, even back then, Jack's income was relatively high. His life was stable and secure. Perhaps, if he had continued along this road, he would not have gone on to cause a stir across the globe. As a middle- to upper-class individual in Hangzhou, with plenty of income to spare, Jack Ma should have been content with his lot. But this was not in his nature. Even Zhang Ying, his life partner, said: "No one knows what idea he is going to come up with next."

After he met Bill, Jack Ma was full of new inspiration and ideas, and soon found a new destination on his voyage. One day when they were chatting, Bill told Jack Ma about a mysterious new thing that had emerged called 'the Internet'. The birth and usage of this enigmatic thing had the potential to reduce the planet we humans lived on down to the size of a village.

For instance, using the internet, two people on opposite sides of the vast Pacific Ocean could talk face to face about their experiences and share their knowledge. The internet could bring about a new era. What kind of era? Bill wiped his mouth. He sounded uncertain when he said it was probably "an information era".

An unfathomable emotion made Jack Ma unable to sit still in his chair. He paced up and down the room with his wine in one hand, shaking his other fist in the air, talking non-stop about the future of the internet; he had a kind of premonition about the information era that was soon to arrive.

Even though he had never seen the mysterious internet for himself, he realized that it was going to change the world and people's lives. He imagined the rapid transmission of information, messages being sent within milliseconds. It would give mankind an entirely new sense. The impact it was going to have on human society could not be overestimated.

The next stop on his voyage of discovery took form. It was the internet. Despite the fact that he had only a vague premonition to guide him, it was a premonition that was real and true. Whenever a prime opportunity like this came about, he would soon turn it into reality. When Bill had left, he could not sleep for a long time. He discussed this mysterious thing with Zhang Ying. They imagined longingly what it would be like if they could bring it to Hangzhou, into people's daily lives.

It would make obtaining information more rapid and up to date. It would make communication simpler and it would be easier to share the fruits of human civilization. It would increase the pace of social progress and social integration. This is what Jack Ma believed.

Zhang Ying leaned against Jack Ma, listening to the sound of his heartbeat. She knew that the man she loved had yet another new idea. Ying had already perceived from the look in his eyes that he was set on a new destination. In Ying's eyes, Jack Ma was a ship. She had built their home into a harbour where Jack's ship would come for fresh water and supplies before inevitably setting off on the next voyage.

Zhang Ying felt that Jack's next destination was without a doubt the internet that Bill had mentioned. Yet where would the opportunity come from? It must be remembered that the internet was still a very unfamiliar concept to Chinese people. Yet fate played its hand and soon after, a chance came about.

––––––––

During the opening-up period, China was still feeling its way through the dark. With the front door flung wide open, foreign waters flooded in. It was hard to sift the good from the bad in such a ferocious torrent. Hangzhou was going to build an expressway all the way to Fuyang in Anhui Province, to the northwest of

Zhejiang, which was going to have a transformative effect on transport in Zhejiang, speeding up logistics and promoting economic development.

The expressway was another product of the opening up, for it was the result of foreign investment. It was a joint equity project. The profits were to be divided up between shareholders. An American businessman provided the capital for this project and when he arrived in Hangzhou, he was met with a warm reception at the Zhejiang Department of Communications.

Zhejiang had been a fertile land since ancient times. A large proportion of the nation's taxes came from Zhejiang, as it was blessed with a rich natural ecosystem and the Yangtze River Delta provided convenient transport links. Building an expressway would enhance Zhejiang's natural conditions and stimulate its economy even further.

The contract was quickly signed and once the land had been acquired and several thousand Communications Department workers had been organized, work started on the expressway.

However, during the construction process, the investor's promised payments were delayed, and there was no way for the construction to continue. Who was going to pay the wages of several thousand workers?

If the Chinese officials were to communicate with the investor, it had to be in English. He claimed not to understand a single word of Chinese, which meant that the situation could not be resolved by making international telephone calls to him. Feeling rather helpless, the Zhejiang Department of Communications sought out Jack Ma.

"Comrade Ma, we hope that you can communicate with the foreign investor on our behalf. Our objective is to hold him to the conditions of the contract and get the promised funds on time." The officials solemnly placed the relevant documents into Jack Ma's hands.

However, the investor was ultimately in breach of the agreement. He agreed to go with Jack Ma to Hong Kong to meet his board of directors, who had to be involved on a decision regarding such a large sum. "Ma," he said, " you'll have no problem persuading our board of directors. Everyone will be convinced by your eloquent way of speaking. I believe in you. Only you can do this."

Flattery is always an effective weapon. On the one hand, Jack Ma felt helpless; on the other, he was really rather confident in his speaking skills. How much more confident would he feel if he managed to persuade the board members in Hong Kong to invest in the Hangzhou to Fuyang expressway?

Thereupon, Jack Ma decided to fly to Hong Kong, with the approval of the Communications Department. In 1995, the Union Jack still flew in the sky above Victoria Bay in Hong Kong. The Pearl of the East was still imbued with the Chinese people's feelings of shame and disgrace due to historical events. When Jack Ma passed through customs, he looked up and saw the throng of traffic on Kowloon Island, in the final days of colonial prosperity. The British colonizers were preoccupied with withdrawing from this overseas administrative enclave that had once brought them great profits.

The investor took Jack Ma to the hotel where he would be staying. After that, there was much aimless rushing around. Either one board member was not present, or a meeting could not be held in their office. It was a rather unusual period in which many people were busy preparing to leave Hong Kong. They did not have time to look into some expressway far away in Hangzhou.

This situation meant that even with his speaking skills, Jack Ma was powerless as there was no one to listen to him. Coming to Hong Kong had been a complete waste of time. Hence, Jack Ma strongly suggested that they return to Hangzhou. There, circumstances had deteriorated severely. It was almost the end of the year. Many tens of thousands of workers still had not been paid. The expressway was in danger of being left half-finished. The distressed officials at the Department of Communications seemed to have reached the end of their tether with the foreign investor. Yet they were able to persuade the officials to approve Jack Ma and the investor going to America and talk with the board of directors there.

America felt a million miles away to Jack Ma. He knew that many thousands of workers' hopes were resting on him and that the Department of Communications had invested their trust in him.

Arrangements had been made for every stage of their journey, from transport to a welcoming dinner. There was even a private villa for Jack Ma to stay in.

Jack Ma slept soundly in the bright and spacious villa. The next day, he quietly prepared his script for the meeting with the board of directors. He wanted to win them over so that the expressway from Hangzhou to Fuyang could be as successful as possible. Zhejiang's provincial government would certainly keep their promise and ensure that the investor and the board were given a percentage of the profits as agreed in the contract at the best possible rate.

During his time in America, Jack Ma was left alone. He ate his meals in solitude and began to feel anxious and irritated. He doubted the legitimacy of the investor and decided that he needed to leave. But he only had 25 cents in his pocket, and it was difficult to do anything with no money in a capitalist society. With no other options to hand, Jack Ma walked into a casino. Here, the neon lights blazed all night long. The entertainment never stopped. Traffic flowed constantly, and the bright lights of the hotels, restaurants and clubs formed a latticework around the other buildings. Breathtaking fountains cast countless drops of water into the air where they were turned into an array of scattered pearls by the multicoloured lights. There was no darkness here, apart from people's shadows. Here, people with money enjoyed themselves to their heart's content, throwing money away recklessly. There was only an endless pursuit of pleasure here with no respite.

A large number of wealthy individuals came here to enjoy themselves. They could recline on luxurious sofas and watch all kinds of exciting performances. They could savour fine wine from all corners of the globe. Under the spinning lights, they made endless extravagant demands. However, to enjoy any of this, you had to have money. Jack Ma only had 25 cents.

All Jack Ma could do was pray for good luck. Resolutely, he walked towards a slot machine. The machine opened its mouth wide and mercilessly swallowed up his money. It did not smile or cry. It was neither thankful nor moved. This was a fine example of modern engineering. Everything was under a form of invisible control. One by one, Jack Ma took his remaining 20 cents and inserted them into the mouth of the slot machine. One cent after another, the machine remained unmoved. The coins it gobbled up remained in its belly. Its eyes did not even blink.

A child next to him laughed. The lights above him flickered. Perhaps, in that moment, Jack Ma was thinking of a distant shore, of his agency Haibo. He let out a long sigh. His feelings of depression seemed to find a release. He shook the coins in his hand. The cents were hard and cold against his palm. He continued to insert them into the machine. Perhaps it was a bottomless pit, for it made no sound when they dropped down.

He got to the 23rd coin. There were only two cents left in his hand. He looked at the slot machine again. Its greedy mouth was stretched wide open. It certainly had an astounding appetite. It had unfeelingly consumed such a large number of coins.

Jack Ma furiously rammed one of his last remaining coins into the machine. Suddenly, it began to make a noise. The lights flashed. The child beside him called out: "You've won, you've won!"

Of course, Jack Ma had no trouble understanding the child's English. His eyes opened wide in delight. Sure enough, the machine shook. Maybe it pitied him. After a series of gurgling sounds, it spat out 600 dollars!

It really was a miracle. Jack Ma had gained 600 dollars with just 25 cents. It was as if he had been brought back from the dead. He ran out of the casino without looking back.

Jack Ma did not hesitate in getting out of there. He had seen through the investor's façade and his only desire was to run away as soon as possible. Without delay, he went and bought a ticket to Seattle with the 600 dollars in his pocket.

When he got on the plane, he fastened his seat belt and let out a long sigh of relief. Jack Ma had finally won back his freedom after a long month of struggle. Soaring up into the blue sky, he drank the in-flight coffee and realized how precious freedom was. He was free to soar, to land – free to make a phone call to his old friend Bill in Seattle. Jack Ma had finally managed to escape a difficult situation due to his resourcefulness and a bit of good luck.

———

Bill was as friendly on the phone as ever and was pleased to hear of Jack Ma's safe landing in Seattle. He was not in town at that time, but immediately sent his son-in-law straight to the airport to pick his friend up.

Jack Ma was moved. It was true: any crowd of people always had a diverse range of characters in it. Not all Chinese people were the same, and this was true for Americans too.

In Seattle, Bill's son-in-law welcomed Jack Ma as cordially as Bill himself. He arranged a place for him to stay so that he could get some good rest.

After some rest, Jack Ma felt that his energy levels had returned to normal. A question began to swirl around in his mind. It was a matter that had been bothering him for a long time: the internet. It seemed that regardless of whether they were good or bad, everyone was drawn to the internet. If this was the case, what was the internet exactly? Jack Ma resolved that, since he had been given the opportunity to come to America, he was not going to leave until he had figured this question out. Perhaps it was his sense of intuition at work again.

He made a request to Bill's son-in-law, who proceeded to laugh heartily. "Well, very well. Come with me." Bill's son-in-law supported Jack Ma's idea. He took him to an internet company and showed him a row of computers, saying: "Come, Jack Ma, have a go. The internet is fantastic. You can basically use it to find whatever you are looking for."

Jack Ma was both surprised and apprehensive. He thought: "I'm scared of even touching the keyboard. Who knows how much this thing is worth! I won't be able to afford to replace it if I break it." It was the first time Jack Ma had had any contact with the internet in his life.

There is no way to prove whether or not he was the first person in China to come into contact with the internet, but it is certain that there was a very small number of people who had access to it at that time. After going through an experience very much like that which Alibaba faced with the 40 thieves, he had finally found the internet that he had longed for day and night. All he had to guide him at that time was an indistinct feeling. He could never have expected that when Alibaba had become a world-famous internet company many years later, people would be certain that it was not a mere feeling, but rather the foresight of a true entrepreneur.

CHAPTER

3

CASTING
OFF

JACK MA & ALIBABA

'Beer'. With the help of Bill's son-in-law, Jack Ma carefully typed out this word using the keyboard. Then he pressed 'Search' using the search engine. Not long afterwards, the names of five companies appeared on the monitor. While there were both American and German companies in the list, there were no Chinese ones. Jack Ma thought it rather strange. He had the impression that China's Qingdao and Yanjing beers were both well known. How come they were not on there? He thought for a while before typing 'Chinese beer'.

Nothing showed up. He then typed 'Chinese history'. This time, a simple and extremely short introduction to the topic appeared on Yahoo. This sparked Jack Ma's interest. The friend of Bill's son-in-law, who had set up the website himself, was very patient in explaining to him that there were currently no websites made in China. There was no one making web pages in China either. "You have to create a web page and upload your company or workplace's information onto it. Then you need to add it to the search engine. This will make it show up if people search for related word groups." Furthermore, the friend offered to upload his company's information and see what happened if he searched for it.

Jack Ma was captivated. He entrusted the friend to make a web page for his translation agency, Haibo. Of course, the hastily produced website was not very enticing and did not even have any decent pictures. It consisted merely of a text introduction, the names of Haibo's staff, and details of the services Haibo offered. At best, it was a simple text-based advert.

He had his new friend upload it onto the internet. Thereupon, the internet gave birth to the first Chinese website, which was called Haibo. If there was a Guinness record for this, it would go to Jack Ma's website for Haibo, for it was the first time a Chinese company's website had been registered online.

Jack Ma did not think much about this move at the time. It was like a casual punch made when practising Tai Chi. Yet it was precisely because of this move that Jack Ma received a call from his new friend at midday, just three hours after the website had been uploaded: "Come and look quickly! There are already five emails." Jack Ma was out shopping at the time, but as soon as he heard the news he raced back to find there really were five emails. They had been sent from America, Japan, and Europe. Some were from companies and others were from international students. One of the emails said: "You are the first ever Chinese website we have seen. Where are you based? We would like to talk business with you."

Jack Ma felt as if he had been knocked over by a huge wave. He could feel his heart pounding in his chest. Even though it seemed that he had made the move carelessly, in actual fact the idea of the internet had been circling round like an eagle in his mind ever since he had discussed it with Bill. Now, after coming in contact with the real thing and taking action, the eagle had landed on his shoulder. He could see its shining feathers and eager eyes. He could hear it saying to him: "Come on, Jack Ma, I will carry you up into the sky, to soar over the oceans and the earth."

It is said that the martial arts character Jack Ma admired the most was Feng Qingyang. Just like Feng Qingyang, he liked to make moves undetectably but gain tangible results. Perhaps that undetected move he had made that day was actually the result of many years of effort, the condensing of his perceptions, a leap in his perceptiveness. In any case, he immediately sensed that this simple event held innumerable business opportunities in store.

He could collect information on all China's domestic businesses and upload them onto a professional website where they would be published for all the world to see. By charging an intermediary fee, he could make a profit. Jack Ma immediately leapt into action. He told his new American friend: "Let's go into business together. You can be in charge of technology. I will return to China to set up the company." The American friend said enthusiastically, "OK!"

In that moment, the initial plan for the world's first B2B e-commerce model was born. Jack Ma did as he set out to do. He used his remaining dollars to buy a 386 computer. Then he flew back over the ocean to Hangzhou. When he arrived, he wasted no time in organizing a meeting.

In reality, it could hardly be called a meeting. Apart from his wife Zhang Ying, all the attendees were his friends and students. In total, there were 24 people present. They were the friends Jack Ma had accumulated over the years. Someone once said that friendship is like putting savings away: just like having savings in the bank, it gives you a sense of fulfilment and a sense of warmth, like sunshine.

Surrounded by 24 of his friends in his own home, Jack Ma felt a warmth rise inside him. He felt grateful for what he had and confident about the future. With great fervour, he began his explanation of what the internet was. Once again, he showed off his speaking skills. His 24 friends suddenly became his students. He explained a brand new concept to them which had the potential to change the entire world. He hoped that they would be just as enchanted by what he had to say as in the past. He hoped that he would be able to persuade them to join him to get involved in a totally foreign but greatly promising idea, and set up China's first ever internet venture.

He was completely animated, his expression full of fire. This was potentially the most exciting lesson he had given in all the six years he had served as a professor at the electrical engineering college. At least, that was what he thought.

When his mouth became dry, he took a glass of water that Zhang Ying passed up to him and took the opportunity to survey his audience. What he saw greatly surprised him. He had never seen people with such blank expressions and so unfocused after he had spoken. There were even a few people who were absent-mindedly looking out of the window. How could Professor Ma put up with this? He finally got straight to the point and asked them directly: "What does everyone think?"

Everyone, including Zhang Ying, looked at each other in dismay. After what seemed like years had passed, someone asked: "Jack Ma, everything you said seems pretty sound, but isn't it a bit early? Not even the government has got involved in this yet. It would be risky to take the first plunge into the deep end."

"That's right!" said another. "Nowhere in China has this thing yet. What are you planning to do?"

It seemed that no one was willing to take on board what he thought was a very enthralling speech. No one realized what an amazing thing this was. But Jack Ma could not be dissuaded. He turned to his last resort: holding a vote. In the end, out of the 24 people there, 23 voted in opposition. Only one person said, "We can have a go. If it doesn't work out we can just give up."

Jack's friends had rejected his presentation about the internet and his proposal to set up a Chinese website. In the midst of this opposition, the meeting came to an end. One by one, people left. Jack Ma kept one person behind, the one person who had not voted against his idea. His name was He Yibing.

Jack Ma did not sleep a wink that night. Zhang Ying did not say anything. Even though she was one of the people who had voted in opposition, she did not want to interrupt Jack's thoughts.

The next day, the sun rose in the east as usual, but Jack Ma had already returned from his morning exercises a while before. Zhang Ying noticed that he was energized and sprightly. She realized that he had already made a decision on the matter.

The first thing Jack Ma did was to submit a letter of resignation to the principal of the college. No one at the college of electrical engineering had expected Jack Ma would to do something like this. His letter of resignation caught them quite unprepared, for they had already arranged a new post for him as head of their foreign affairs department.

In September 1995, Jack Ma resigned from his job. He happened to have just turned 30. Over the years, he had accumulated some business knowledge and sufficient contacts. The time had come for him to make a brave leap. He was setting sail on the vast blue ocean with the Ma flag flying high. Jack Ma left his ivory tower with not a single look back. There was certainly an unpredictable and merciless world of business awaiting him, but he dived right in and begun fighting the current. He gave up everything he had. He scrimped and saved 6,000 yuan, borrowed several tens of thousands from his family and friends, sold some of the equipment at Haibo Translation Agency and the shares of two shareholders. In total, he pieced together 100,000 yuan. He set up China's first ever commercial website, China Yellow Pages. The name of the company was Zhejiang Haibo Internet Technology Company Limited.

The company initially had three employees: the manager Jack Ma, the assistant manager He Yibing, and staff member Zhang Ying. The work was divided so that the two managers, Jack Ma and He Yibing, were responsible for going out on business and finding clients while Ying stayed and looked after the office.

Jack Ma and his wife had invested 80,000 yuan in the company's shares, while He Yibing had put up

10,000, and a third shareholder, Song Weixing, had also given 10,000.

In an explosion of firecracker smoke, China's first internet company opened for business in beautiful Hangzhou. The only piece of equipment that the company owned was the 386 computer that Jack Ma had brought back from the United States. It was a rather wretched situation, but at the time even a computer like that was a real rarity. Jack Ma swiftly taught Zhang Ying how to use the computer by herself. Her main task was to send emails. Jack Ma went out into the marketplace with He Yibing, publicizing internet marketing and promoting e-commerce.

And so, like a small boat tossed about in the wind and rain, this unfamiliar e-commerce marketing company that no one understood, or was even aware of, set off into the boundless ocean with the slight-framed Jack Ma at its helm.

Looking back at these events in hindsight, Jack Ma had more praise for his bravery than his keen business sense. He said, "I had seen this thing that I really wanted to imitate. Many young people dream of many fantastic paths they could take before they sleep at night, but when they get up in the morning they still continue on the same road. The most important thing about setting up a new business in China is not whether or not you have an outstanding idea, ideal, or dream. What's most important is whether or not you are willing to pay a price for it and whether or not you are willing to give your all to prove that you were right.

"What really made me most determined was not my confidence in the internet, but rather my belief that every experience is a kind of success. You have to make a dash for it. If it doesn't work out you can always turn around. Yet if you never try, you are just another one of those people who takes the same road every morning and never realizes any of the paths they envisage before sleep."

In 1995, Jack Ma was not the only person to have ever come into contact with the internet. Even in China, there were plenty of people who knew what the internet was and had had dealings with it. However, Jack Ma was probably the only person among them who took action the moment he saw it. Hence, China Yellow Pages enjoyed the reputation of being China's first online e-commerce platform.

The company had been registered and the website was up and running. However, Hangzhou remained without internet connection until the fourth month of China Yellow Pages doing business. How could a website keep running if it could not connect to the internet?

First of all, they translated documentation containing information about Chinese companies (including photos with captions) into English. Then, they posted these to Seattle. Their friends in America assisted them by transforming them into web pages and uploading them. Following on from that, they printed the web pages in colour and sent them back to Hangzhou. China Yellow Pages took the printed web pages to the respective companies for their inspection and informed them that they had successfully been registered on the internet. If their clients were sceptical, then they would be given the home page's web address and the phone number in Seattle so they could make an enquiry.

Jack Ma's China Yellow Pages charged a standard fee of 20,000 to 30,000 yuan for this complicated process. The operation wasted time, money, and a large amount of manpower. In terms of time, it took them about two weeks to turn around one job. Moneywise, the asking price for international postage was quite considerable. Most crucially, there was no internet in Hangzhou at the time. No one knew anything about the internet. No one believed in the Internet or imagined that you could do business with something so intangible. And even though it was Jack Ma's side of the operation that was making the most effort in gathering clients, it was the American side which took 60% of the earnings, leaving Jack's company with just 40%.

It would not have been unreasonable to swap the percentages around. American people were already well acquainted with the internet. They were used to making websites to provide information about products. This meant that there was a wide client base in America. They would have ample means to survive and develop even if they gave away a portion of their profits. China, on the other hand, was still conducting traditional business. Moreover, Chinese people hated to break old habits.

Even the advertising industry had only appeared very recently. At least with an advert in a newspaper or on the television you could see it was real with your own eyes, regardless of how good it was; customers felt reassured. The internet, on the other hand, felt rather intangible. If all they got to see was a colour print-out of their company introduction after they had put up an advert, many business owners would shake their heads in firm rejection. It seemed that the internet was ahead of its time. Even though it was a remarkable thing, people were not ready for it yet.

But Jack Ma would not be dissuaded. He decided to leave the most challenging tasks till last. First of all, he sought out companies that he had already had dealings with in the past and was on friendly terms with. He looked to open up the market with his personal contacts, family, and friends. He began by making websites for companies that had previously done business with Haibo Translation Agency. If they had the money to pay for them, he would take it; but if they did not have enough, he would make it free.

The first companies online were Hangzhou Lakeview Guesthouse, Hangzhou Second Television Factory, and a law firm that had had dealings with Haibo in the past. These firms began to receive telephone calls and faxes from abroad soon after, which proved that the websites made by Jack Ma and his friends in America were effective. The idea for China Yellow Pages to put Chinese businesses on the global stage was finally being realized. However, company directors still did not buy the idea because they could not see their web page in real life. It was a great shame that Hangzhou did not have the internet at that time.

Jack Ma felt as though the days were dragging by like years. When would the internet make it to Hangzhou?

He knew that day would have to come eventually, because ultimately people could not deny the need for it.

In July 1995, Shanghai went online. Jack Ma was one of the first people to find out. He was overjoyed and immediately went out to buy a 486 computer, which was relatively powerful at the time. He used a long-distance phone connection to link up with the internet in Shanghai. Once online, he searched for the home page of the Hangzhou Lakeview Guesthouse website that his friends in America had made. The connection was so slow that it took him a whole three hours to do so. Gradually, the home page of the Lakeview Guesthouse appeared in front of his eyes.

Jack Ma stood straight up and pointed at the computer: "Look, look!"

People soon began to recognize and accept the internet. They realized what it was capable of, and began to look upon Jack Ma in a favourable light. China Yellow Pages finally had an income.

However, Jack Ma only took 8,000 of the 20,000 yuan they made from the first sale, because the American side was still entitled to 60% of the profits according to the agreement. Yet Jack Ma and his coworkers could now see light on the horizon. They redoubled their efforts to publicize the internet, not just in Hangzhou, but in 27 cities all round China.

Jack Ma reminded himself that, "The internet will influence people's lives for many years to come. To keep up on the marathon that is the evolution of the internet, you must run as fast as a rabbit but have the patience of a tortoise."

Jack Ma was distrusted in cities that were not online. No one took any notice of him. Some even avoided him. However, Jack Ma would not be beaten. Like a man possessed, he kept on talking to them non-stop about the internet and e-commerce. He managed to persuade business owners and journalists.

One owner of a company in Hangzhou insisted that e-commerce was a trick designed to deceive people, even after Jack Ma had called upon him five times.

Thereupon, Jack Ma decided to send him a large collection of documents containing information on e-commerce. He took the time to patiently explain to the business owner that e-commerce was a new kind of business model. The internet had coverage all over the world. It connected every single household together. For this reason, it was much more effective to advertise on the internet than on any other form of media.

Even though Jack Ma was rather proud of his ability to persuade people and he listed many examples, the business owner was still rather sceptical. Anyone else might have given up and gone home, ending it there. Jack Ma, however, was different from other people. He was not willing to give up on this tough old bone which could bring him extra business if he gnawed away at it. As a result, he decided to collect some files on the company. A few days later, he turned up there with a notebook computer.

Jack Ma loaded the computer's search engine in front of the business owner. Not long after, the company's information gradually appeared on the screen. Jack Ma told him that any computer in any location could see the same information that they were seeing now. It would be just as effective regardless of whether the person accessing it was in America, China, or any other part of the world. This was the internet. This was the miraculous e-commerce he had been talking about.

There is a saying in Chinese, quite fitting in this case, which translates into something like the English "Seeing is believing." Finally, Jack Ma's efforts were beginning to have some success in this period when the internet was just beginning to find its feet. The business owner finally paid the fee to China Yellow Pages.

Jack Ma was praised for his unflagging efforts and tenacious spirit in seeking out new customers. China Yellow Pages found it gained more of a reputation as a result. More people learned what the internet was after hearing the story.

From Lakeview Guesthouse to Hangzhou Second Television Factory, from Qianjiang lawyers to Wuxi Little Swan (a brand of domestic appliances) and Guoan Football Club in Beijing, China Yellow Pages began to expand out from Hangzhou across the country.

China Central Television still has in its archives a feature programme about Jack Ma and the internet called *Jack Ma the Bookworm*, filmed by a reporter from Hangzhou called Fan Xinman.

Let us first examine the term 'bookworm'. There are two Chinese sayings which go: "Bookworms have no use in the real world" and "Intellectuals cannot achieve anything even if they revolt for three years on end." In Chinese culture, the words 'bookworm' and 'intellectual' have similar meanings. The sayings mean that studious people are unlikely to achieve anything of great importance. If you read too much, you will lose touch with reality, leading you to stubbornly pursue foolish matters.

Bookworms are usually found in schools and are mostly either students or teachers. They either talk about knowledge or study it. Overall, a bookworm tends to be a bit stubborn, a bit aloof, and detached from world affairs. It is clear from the moment the camera starts filming that Jack Ma is talking nineteen to the dozen, spittle flying in all directions, about how he is going to build China's biggest library of information so that Chinese companies can enter the international stage. He has a shrewd expression on his face, while everyone watching looks rather blank. They are devoid of trust or enthusiasm and even have no questions about what he is saying. It is like a group of people listening to an alien talk about another planet. This was the reception Jack Ma met with in Beijing that year. It was a reception pretty similar to the one the internet met with when it first came to China.

———

The year 1995 was a significant one: it was the year when the internet came to China. Just like anything which has vitality, it took off like a whirlwind as soon as it arrived, engulfing the entire nation. People like Charles Zhang, Wang Zhidong and Chen Tianqiao, who later became big shots in the internet world, had already gone into business. Internet Technologies China (ITC), later called Sohu, founded by Charles Zhang, and Chinese Star, founded by Wang Zhidong, became well known across China as the internet spread.

Chen Tianqiao had already joined the Lujiazui Group which already had some dealings with the internet. It is true that information is not exclusive to anyone. It cannot be kept secret. Anyone knowledgeable and perceptive with a certain amount of business sense will home in on it immediately. It should be acknowledged that there were many people who were as knowledgeable and experienced as Jack Ma.

China Yellow Pages was threatened by this fact. It had only just started making a profit. It was still just a young seedling. If China Yellow Pages did not fight for more room to develop, then it would be difficult for it to ever see daylight again once other internet companies had grown up into tall trees, blocking out the light. The threat posed by other companies made Jack Ma aware of another issue: Hangzhou was too small, not in terms of the city itself, but in terms of its power to influence.

In response, after some discussion, Jack Ma and his shareholders decided to advance on Beijing, the centre of China's political, economic, and cultural spheres. They had to move there. From there, they would have the power to climb high and reach out to the entire nation. It would provide the necessary conditions for China Yellow Pages to develop swiftly into a towering tree.

Therefore, Jack Ma and his partners moved north to the capital. They would be beside the imperial city and find their footing in Beijing. Backed by the entire nation, they could march towards the international stage. This was Jack Ma's new dream, his new strategy. Upon their arrival, he immediately got a positive feeling about this strategy.

Beijing was huge. Countless ring roads expanded out from the centre, which was home to every kind of ministry, commission, office, embassy, and consulate. You could tell at a glance that this was an international city.

In the beginning, Jack Ma had dreamed of being one of the first Chinese people to set up a top global company and build one of the top ten websites worldwide. When he got to Beijing, he was struck by this feeling once again. There was space to expand here. He began working frenetically, spreading the word as far as he could. This was the period when that special feature *Jack Ma the Bookworm* was filmed.

At the time Jack Ma was still unaware that there was great contention about the internet among higher levels of society and that there were two opposing sides which met squarely on the issue. One side said that China must not expand the freeway of information, or it would fall under the control of developed Western nations. The other side, however, felt that China had to develop its internet infrastructure or it would be cut off from the information age by a digital gulf.

What effect would the crazy efforts of Jack Ma the bookworm have when this debate was still ongoing? The media were not willing to take on the task of reporting on the internet while the leadership still had not expressed their stance on the matter. Jack Ma decided to follow a rather unusual method. He sought out the head of a media company and slipped him some files on China Yellow Pages, as well as a finished article and 500 yuan in cash. Five hundred yuan was worth a lot back then. Jack Ma said: "It did not matter which media outlet it was. As soon as it was published, it belonged to you."

The head of the said company was also rather unusual. He published the article successively on five different media outlets, including *China Trade News*, where it made the front page. Jack Ma discovered he had a friend out there. He immediately paid a visit to the editor-in-chief of *China Trade News*. The two men regretted not having met one another earlier, and went on to discuss matters for two days straight. Looking back, Jack Ma recalled: "Just like me, he did not understand the internet at that time, but was of the firm belief that it had potential. He said, 'Jack Ma, I support you.'"

The editor-in-chief took Jack Ma to visit the person in charge of the State Information Centre, but their enthusiasm fell on deaf ears. The director's eyes drifted around the room as he spoke, and he gave several hints as to what his opinion on the matter was. Jack Ma heard him loud and clear: how could a grand institution like the State Information Centre consider working with a private firm? Jack Ma had met with a rebuff.

Despite this, Jack Ma did not lose heart; giving up was not in his nature. With help from his sympathizers and supporters, he paid successive visits to many ministries and departments, including the Ministry of Culture and the State Physical Culture and Sports Commission. However, in 1995, privately run businesses had little influence.

Furthermore, Jack Ma's China Yellow Pages was just a small website situated far away in the Yangtze River Delta. Its gross profit was just one million yuan, which was a pittance in Beijing, especially in the eyes of the officials working for central government ministries. The notion of their working with Jack Ma was absurd. The feature *Jack Ma the Bookworm* records this period of time when he had run into a wall.

According to the reporter Fan Xinman, who filmed the feature: "He comes across as a baddie on camera. He always has a cunning look on his face, despite the fact he is always talking. He keeps going on about what he is planning to do, about how he is going to build the biggest library of information in China. However, if you look at the expressions of people in the audience, then you can tell that no one has a clue what he is talking about."

Despite this, Jack's non-stop talking did manage to influence a few educated people, including Ms Fan Xinman. The feature made it onto *Oriental Horizon*, a major programme on China Central Television.

Print media, especially central state media, has great influence in China.

Because of Jack Ma and the educated people that he was able to influence, things began to change for the better. When the information department of the *People's*

Daily newspaper heard about Jack Ma, they invited him to give a speech. Of course, he accepted: he never gave up an opportunity to speak. Faced with the opinions of the head of an authoritative media outlet and scholars from several institutes of engineering, Jack Ma got rather worked up and indignant, saying, "China got on the last bus compared to other developing nations. It missed a rare opportunity that might not come again. We are in a disadvantaged position, so our best chance at defending ourselves is to go on the offensive."

Jack Ma spoke with passion and flair, but he spoke very rationally. Several scholars from the institutes of engineering believed that the internet did not suit China's national conditions. Jack Ma ruthlessly criticized these ignorant 'experts'. He pointed out that the internet was going to create a revolution in human history. It was a momentous discovery. If they sealed off the country and avoided contact with the outside world, then they would lose out on yet another opportunity for China to develop. The media outlet's staff, who had broader perspectives and experience, applauded at what Jack Ma said. Jack Ma knew how much their applause was worth. With tears in his eyes, he gave them a glance which conveyed his gratitude.

Fan Jingyi, who was then the chief editor of the *People's Daily*, made a profound comment on Jack's speech. He was a rather strict and serious academic. He realized that the internet was quickly going to explode and engulf the world of the future. The next day, he sent a report to the central authorities requesting permission for the *People's Daily* to register online.

There is another story behind this. The editor of *China Trade News* organized a news conference for Jack Ma in the Ledger Dining Hall of the Chang An Club. The aim of the conference was to seek out business partners for China Yellow Pages in Beijing. Over 30 media outlet heads and several successful real-estate investors attended. Jack Ma and his technical staff spent a long time preparing for the event, but before the date even came around, they were informed that documents from higher leadership had been distributed and that they were not allowed to promote the internet. Jack Ma and his technical staff were left in dismay. It seemed their good luck had run out. They picked out a few documents that might still be useful.

The news conference still convened on time. Jack Ma and his technical staff set up a computer and a telephone connection. They displayed the home page of China Yellow Pages live. Next, Jack Ma went on stage and gave a passionate, yet clear and logical speech. He spoke for over an hour on topics ranging from the internet's usage to its future. However, the guests and reporters who attended the meeting only seemed to understand half of what he said and were left rather baffled.

After the dinner, the host sought out two real-estate executives to introduce to Jack Ma. He still hoped that Jack Ma would be able to obtain the support of a powerful figure. Only with that kind of support would he have a chance at turning his dream into reality.

Jack Ma drummed up some courage and explained his ideas to them once again. He spoke for over an hour non-stop. The two executives seemed to have got the idea; however, they had a question: "Would the state let privately run enterprises get involved in something like this?" Jack Ma was stumped. After all, at the time the higher leadership still had not made their stance on the internet clear.

Not long after, the request by the *People's Daily* to register online was approved. This was a startling piece of information, given the status of that newspaper. If the *People's Daily* was going to go online, then it proved that the internet was inevitably going to expand in China.

In that moment, all previous obstructions seemed to disperse overnight. The internet was going to be popular in Beijing and across China. Perhaps this was a chance for China Yellow Pages to ride with the tide and launch itself.

Jack Ma was able to keep a cool head. He had already noted that large numbers of foreign enterprises, with considerable financial and technological backing, would flock to China if the internet could break through the barriers set up against it. But China Yellow Pages had neither the capital nor any powerful backers. There were too many competitors for Jack Ma to establish himself, survive and expand in these rapidly developing circumstances.

Could he defeat his rivals? Jack Ma thought it over that evening while making some calculations. How much would it cost him to rent a retail space in Beijing? What processes would he have to undergo in order to get a licence? What connections and workers could he rely on? As Jack Ma meticulously calculated the answers to these questions, he felt increasingly calm. Trusting his own calculations, he concluded that there was no opportunity for him to progress any further in Beijing.

Jack Ma probably subconsciously realized at that point that he was going to have to rely on the small to medium enterprises found in his native Zhejiang Province. Of course, he was only vaguely aware of this fact at that point. Yet he knew that China Yellow Pages could not permanently move to Beijing, for it would very likely be squeezed out by the forest of powerful competitors there. As a result, he decided to return home to Hangzhou.

However, the internet business scene had already undergone great changes in Hangzhou in the short period that they had spent in Beijing. As soon as the internet gained approval, internet companies and websites began to spring up everywhere. No one in the world could claim to be better than Chinese people at imitating others.

The internet scene in Hangzhou had already erupted into a raging conflict. First there was east.net and AsiaInfo.com, then there was West Lake Network. Just like the Cultural Revolution period, it seemed as if hordes of squadrons had appeared on the scene overnight, all with outstanding fighters vying for victory.

The size of the market had not changed; how could it be shared between that many companies? Of course, it was a simple matter of the survival of the fittest. The victorious lived on, while the weak quickly became extinct.

Some people say that the business world is comparable to a battlefield. In reality, the business world is precisely that. In hand-to-hand combat, only the strongest and most valiant warriors can win.

Jack Ma's China Yellow Pages did not lack courage, resources, or teamwork. It certainly did not lack willpower and perseverance. However, the company had no backing or robust capital. In war, strength is what counts, and in this war the essential weapon was money. Jack Ma did not have money! West Lake Network was the most powerful player on Hangzhou's internet scene at that time. It had 300 million yuan in capital and was a subsidiary of China Telecom. From funding to backing, it was obvious that Jack Ma had no chance. China Yellow Pages found itself faced with a giant wielding a great iron hammer. If it lifted its hand, Jack Ma and China Yellow Pages would be hard pressed to defend themselves, to say nothing of going on the offensive.

Moreover, West Lake Network was quite clever in its tactics. It had chosen a name rather similar to China Yellow Pages, which was chinesepage.com in English, only a few letters different from Jack Ma's chinapage. com. Such tricks were a common occurrence in business competition, but were enough to yield results. If Jack Ma had tried to file a lawsuit, then he would have got a shot across the bows from West Lake Network, warning him that if he looked closely, the names were not exactly the same.

There was nothing to be done about it. Every time someone came up with a good brand, it would naturally meet with a similar situation. After a messy battle, Jack Ma's China Yellow Pages was defeated. In an instant, a rather ugly situation reared its head. Not only did they find their market shrunk, but even paying the staff on time became an issue.

Jack Ma had no choice but to agree to a merger. West Lake Network would invest along with China Yellow Pages to set up a new company. Jack Ma's China Yellow Pages had a 30% share of the stocks, while West Lake Network held 70%. That is to say, West Lake Network owned a controlling number of shares in the company without a doubt. From the outside it looked like a cooperative deal but, in reality, China Yellow Pages' development had been curtailed by West Lake Network.

———

Not long after, Jack Ma took his team south to grow their business. After a period of time, they returned to Hangzhou, only to find that the situation there had progressed far beyond their imaginations. China Telecom (one of China's two major mobile phone service providers), to which West Lake Network was subordinate, had made use of its ample capital to specially register a new company. The company was called China Yellow Pages. Moreover, it was carving up the market like there was no tomorrow. If anyone else could set up a web page for 5,000 yuan, they would do it for 1,000.

In November 1997, a damp chill was already creeping through Hangzhou. Winter had arrived in the south. Jack Ma took 40 members of his team from China Yellow Pages to the holiday town of Tonglu, famous for the red lanterns which line its streets. Jack Ma was silent the whole way there. He did not say one word on the bus journey. Perhaps he was feeling tired. Everyone was very understanding: it had been a challenging time for him.

That evening, Jack Ma asked the restaurant they visited to prepare a sumptuous feast for everyone. When they had started eating, Jack Ma slowly rose to his feet. With a grave expression on his face, he began to speak. It was the first time his team had ever seen him speak without his usual passion and fervour. In place of his customary enthusiasm was a terse and clear-cut announcement.

Jack Ma declared that he had decided to resign from his post and return to the capital to make another attempt at getting established there. He also read out a list of the names of eight people who would be going with him. Thereupon, he sank into his seat.

It was so quiet you could have heard a pin drop. After this period of silence had passed, however, the restaurant erupted in a cacophony of noise. No one could have predicted his announcement. Not only was he the founder of China Yellow Pages, he was the heart and soul of the company. What was anyone without their soul?

Everyone was quite aware of what Jack's resignation would mean for China Yellow Pages. No one was willing to let him go. Had the past two years of hardship, trials and tribulations all been for nothing?

Every single person in the room was in an indescribable state of shock. Some people could not help weeping. The atmosphere of the dinner party instantly became rather stifled. Many people requested to join Jack Ma's expedition to the north. Jack Ma steeled himself and said: "I'm afraid that is not possible. China Yellow Pages must go on. If you all leave, what will happen to it?"

To tell the truth, Jack Ma had not made this decision lightly. It was probably the most difficult one he had ever made. After all, China Yellow Pages was like a child to him. He had painstakingly cared for it from its birth and through its infancy. He had invested his all to get it to the point where it could independently take its first steps. However, if he did not leave now, he would have been resigning himself to doing nothing. China Yellow Pages had not taken on board his suggestions. There was no possibility of growth and development there. Even its very survival was at stake.

It was the senior member of China Yellow Pages, He Yibing, who handed in his resignation first. He was furious beyond reconciliation. Then it was Jack Ma's turn. He filed a request to leave the company. At the end of 1997, the e-Commerce Centre of China's Ministry of Foreign Trade sent a heartfelt invitation for Jack Ma to join them in their great undertaking.

He selected eight members of his original team to go with him to Beijing. He then divided his 21% share of the company stocks between the 32 members who were staying behind to take care of things. Jack Ma could not help welling up when faced with these teammates who had stood by him through innumerable hardships in pursuit of their venture. He had never cared much for money. Having given all the stocks in his possession to these companions who had stuck together as a team through hard times, he finally felt at ease. He just hoped that they would continue to work diligently and reap the rewards of their hard work.

Jack Ma was a loyal man. He only took a few talented staff away with him, leaving behind the core members of their team at China Yellow Pages, including their most talented engineers. Jack Ma sincerely hoped that the company would continue to expand and develop. He said, "I left China Yellow Pages just when it was starting to make money. The turnover that year was 7 million. At the end of the day, China Yellow Pages is like a son to me. Whatever happens from now on, I won't do anything to hurt it."

CHAPTER

LEAVING HARBOUR

Badaling, northwest of Beijing. Between the hazy horizon and the undulating peaks, it snaked endlessly across the landscape – magnificent and spectacular, majestic and imposing. There was no mistaking the Beijing section of the Great Wall of China. This section had been the best preserved since its construction hundreds of years ago. Traversing the formidable and lofty Yanshan Mountain range, its exterior was aged but robust. It was a sign for people who came here that the Chinese nation was ancient, rich, and vibrant. It was tenacious and everlasting.

A group of vendors had gathered on one of the guard towers. Jack Ma bought each one of his team a black T-shirt. It was nothing special, but on the front was printed, "He who has not climbed the Great Wall is not a real man." People burst out laughing when they saw it. They seemed to have caught on to what Jack Ma was trying to say.

They had been in Beijing for a year at this point. How time had flown! From China Yellow Pages to China's new found wealth, Jack Ma and his team had undergone a series of great changes in their perspective.

They were welcomed by the Ministry of Foreign Trade upon their arrival in Beijing. Jack Ma assumed the position of general manager of the ministry's website, Guofutong. He had had contact with the Ministry of Foreign Trade previously; he had helped build their previous website. This time, however, he was there in person. He found it completely different from what he had expected.

Jack Ma later admitted that while he was not one to deceive others, he did lie to his colleagues then. He built

Beijing up to be a wonderful place and the Ministry of Foreign Trade to have fantastic prospects. However, the website they were in charge of turned out to be just an internal one, not connected to the internet. The Ministry of Foreign Trade used the internal website to publish official documents. They dealt with state-owned enterprises, which meant they had to do what they were told regardless of what they thought. Money was not a problem.

Jack's heart was not really in it. He wanted to be involved with the internet, with a website that was in sync with the global information network. That way, he could not only find platforms for Chinese enterprises to advertise themselves, but also find openings for global enterprises to set up in China. However, this was just an idea and nothing more. He had no choice but to obey orders and remain where he was. This caused Jack Ma to become more and more depressed.

A year later, they achieved great success. They had launched an online trading platform for Chinese technology exports, an online investment platform, an export commodities fair and a foreign trade site, which was recommended by *Chinese Government Internet Engineering* as an outstanding website for the year 1999.

The online trading platform for Chinese goods was the first time the Chinese government had organized a large scale e-commerce event. Shi Guangsheng, who was head of the Ministry of Foreign Trade at the time, called it "a never-ending trade fair". At the same time, Jack Ma was working in cooperation with Jerry Yang, the co-founder of Yahoo, creating an opportunity for

Guofutong to become the exclusive advertising agent for Yahoo in China. Jack Ma was still able to put on a dazzling performance despite his limited resources. This was just the kind of person he was, never willing to sit idly by. A number of media outlets praised him and his associates, calling them "the dream team".

Indeed, Jack Ma's website, Guofutong, and the trading platform for Chinese goods affiliated to it made a net profit of over 2.8 million yuan that year. This meant that the team members were able to enjoy an increase in their pay. To them, tens of thousands of yuan no longer seemed a big deal.

As a matter of fact, there were advantages to being part of the system. At least, they were rewarded when they produced good results, but did not have to pick up the pieces if they made a loss.

But while there seemed to be a lack of progress within the system, there was definitely plenty of regression. At least wages were protected. Jack Ma himself said that he felt very much like an official. How could the head of a government website in this great nation not be considered an official? However, despite his good position in such a good workplace, Jack Ma could not help feeling depressed and agitated. None of his suggestions were approved and none of his proposals were adopted. He felt very far from his previous dream of being the creator of a globally influential e-commerce platform.

Jack Ma himself said that his goal was never to make money, but rather to do something. It took him a year to realize that the ministry was not the place for him.

After some careful deliberation, Jack Ma, who was always inevitably going to come up with a new idea, made a decision. He gathered the team of people who had come with him to Beijing and made an announcement: "I will give you three choices. First, transfer to Yahoo with my recommendation. Yahoo will take you on without a doubt. Moreover, the salary will be high. Secondly, go to Sina or Sohu [two of China's leading internet companies], where the pay will also be good. Thirdly, return home with me. The pay will only be 800 yuan. You must rent a place within five minutes from where I live, which is where you will come to work. You will not be permitted to take taxis to work. The choice is up to you."

When he had finished speaking, Jack Ma sat down and waited. Like a suspect on trial, he waited for the verdict. The judge was his team, his colleagues, his band of eight people whom he had brought from Hangzhou.

These eight people had followed Jack Ma from the beginning of China Yellow Pages, fighting battles across the country. Not only did they now possess outstanding technical skills, but they were also professional experts when it came to online marketing, customer advertising, and e-commerce development. In addition, after many years of hard work, they had each built up their own personal network of contacts and their own clientele. To put it bluntly, they were the cream of the crop when it came to the internet in China at that time. It would be incredibly difficult to find anyone who understood the internet better, or was more suited to working in an internet company, than them.

Jack Ma was not boasting. He really could give each member of his team a recommendation that would land them a good job and would allow them to remain comfortably in Beijing, thanks to his connections and to each of their personal talents.

When he had finished what he had to say, no one said anything or tried to persuade him, for everyone knew that it would be no use. All they could do was make the choice. Thereupon, they walked out of the room one by one. Jack Ma had given them three days to make the decision whether they wanted to stay in Beijing or go back with him to give it another shot.

As it turned out, it took ten minutes rather than three days. Everyone came back and said in unison, "We will go with you!" In that moment, Jack Ma could not hold back his tears. Was there anything in the world more precious than a moment like this?

Sticking together through hard times, joining hands in the face of adversity, never leaving one another – there were no solemn vows here, no oaths between sworn brothers to die together. The team of eight people just showed by their actions that they were inseparable from one another. They would stay together through thick and thin to create a Chinese e-commerce platform that would shake the world.

It was in that moment that Jack Ma said to himself, "My friends have not let me down. I must never let them down either! We will go back and start again from zero. The company we will build will leave us with no regrets." They handed in their resignations to the Ministry of Foreign Trade together.

———

This was the story behind the day when Jack Ma and his team visited the Great Wall. Badaling was lofty and precipitous. The Great Wall wound up the steep mountain ranges, down through valleys and over peaks. The steps at the steepest part of the wall were almost vertical. By the time they had reached the 'Slope of Heroes', they were all dripping with sweat.

There was a bone-chilling wind whistling up the slope. To the north was the Yanshan Mountain range stretching away forever into the distance, undulating across the landscape. To the south, a purplish mist shrouded the capital, yellow tiles atop dark bricks, hanging beams and arched eaves. Between them and Beijing stood the mountain pass of Juyongguan, majestic and precipitous. It is said that this was where Li Zicheng, the leader of the peasant rebellion that ended the Ming dynasty, broke through the frontier and marched on to Beijing. Everyone who visited his place felt the profound weight of history bearing down and the fleeting nature of human existence. Perhaps it was also possible to hear the beat of galloping hooves and bloodcurdling battle cries. It was hard not to let one's imagination run wild in such a place. Suddenly, one of the team called out, "Why? Why do we give so much but get so little in return!"

Indeed, they had given the most precious period of their lives, but now they had to start again from scratch. What did the future hold for them? Jack Ma did not have any answers at that point. He just promised himself that he would build a website that would make all Chinese people proud. That evening, a thick layer of snow fell on Beijing. They walked into a hotel …

As the snowflakes flurried around them, they struck up a solemn and stirring tune. It was the last night Jack Ma and his team were going to spend in Beijing. There is a precious videotape recording still kept at the headquarters of Alibaba. It is a record of the misery and helplessness, but also enthusiasm and idealism of Jack Ma and his team. It is a record of when they started out on their new undertaking.

On that stormy night they returned south to Hangzhou. After a period of preparation, Jack Ma and his team – now 18 in number, like the 18 Arhats, the original followers of the Buddha.– gathered in his residence on the bank of West Lake. They were meeting to discuss establishing a new company. In addition to the small team Jack Ma had brought back from Beijing, the rest of the 18 people present were his students, colleagues, and friends. To put it simply, they were all people who respected and trusted him and who had worked with him in the world of business before. There was a tacit understanding between them. They had weathered storms together before and were ready to do so again.

Jack Ma spoke with feeling about this matter: "Starting from now, we begin on a grand journey. Our B2B [business to business] solution is going to revolutionize the online service industry. We will fumble together through the darkness. When we find something, we will cry out together. When I call for you to charge ahead, do not panic. What is there to be afraid of when there are a dozen of you marching forward together, armed and ready?"

The internet had already entered a period of surging development at that point. Those Chinese companies that had got a head start, such as Sina, Sohu, and NetEase, were already standing steady on two feet with their banners flying proudly in the sky. Only e-commerce remained in a state of chaos. People were falling over each other in their eagerness to copy Amazon, Yahoo, and other internet giants.

Chinese people's greatest strength and speciality is imitating others. Once an idea has been aired, they can conjure it up in an instant. Innovation and invention, on the other hand, are Chinese people's weakness. Faced with such tasks, they have little to offer. Jack Ma was different. He was an outstanding individual and was not content to follow the trail left by other people. At the Asian E-Commerce Convention, he looked around and found the field to be dominated by Americans and Europeans. He found them to be running Asia on their terms.

At that point, there was still no e-commerce model that was well suited for the Asian market. Thus, it became Jack Ma's goal to build an e-commerce platform that was just that. Day and night, he dreamed of its becoming a reality.

What exactly would this uniquely Chinese-style B2B website be like? Jack Ma explained it like this: "In today's economic world, large corporations are the whales who eat small fish and even kill for a living. The small fry also survive by stealing the whales' leftovers, creating a mutually beneficial relationship.

"The internet industry, however, is a highly individualistic domain. Small enterprises can create their own independent spaces online. The range of goods on offer is more diverse and colourful. This is what makes the internet truly revolutionary. If enterprises were rich and poor people, then the internet would be the kingdom of the poor man, for it costs the same amount of money for a small enterprise to open a page as it does for a large one. I have come here to lead the poor people to revolution."

In short, Jack Ma wanted to build a website for small-to medium-sized enterprises. When he left Beijing, he had already noticed the small to medium enterprises of Zhejiang and the Yangtze River Delta. Hangzhou was their centre; the place to lead from.

At the meeting, of which a recording still exists, Jack Ma took out all the money in his pockets and laid it down on the table before saying, "The only funds we are allowed to put into this endeavour are the spare money we already have. We must not borrow from friends or family, for there is a huge possibility that we will fail. We must be prepared to meet with the worst outcome. However, even if I am knocked down by [US boxing champion] Mike Tyson, I will get up and continue to fight as long as I am not dead." He continued: "Now, make sure that each one of you keeps back a bit of money to eat, and put the rest on the table. Moreover, you can only be team leaders. For the commanders, I'll look for them somewhere else, for I must also learn from the rest of you very qualified individuals."

After a pause he said, "We are going to set up an e-commerce company with three goals:

"Firstly, we will set up a company that will last for a minimum of 80 years.

"Secondly, the company will serve small- to medium-scale Chinese enterprises.

"Thirdly, it will become the biggest e-commerce company in the world, and be ranked among the global top ten websites."

The goals he set were ambitious. His speech made everyone's pulse race. His 18 followers sat around him, eyes shining, full of passion. It was hard to say whether they had truly seen the future of the e-commerce website that was just about to be born, let alone seen it entering the global list of top ten sites. However, they had Jack Ma and that was enough. If he said "top ten", then they might just make it to the top ten.

No one opposed Jack Ma. On the contrary, they showed their support for him by scraping together 500,000 yuan between them. The funds provided fuel for their voyage. Just as if they were about to depart from port, their gazes turned to the surging tide that lay in front of them. A sum of 500,000 yuan did not amount to much, especially if they were going to set up the world's biggest e-commerce company.

There is an Arab legend about riches that is famous across the globe. Arabic culture stretches back as far as the Chinese; they are equally fond of wealth. Their long history is revered in a similar way to China's. They created a myth in which honest, hard-working, and kind Alibaba accidentally came across some treasure during one of his adventures, gleaming with gold, silver and jewels. Henceforth, the name Alibaba became a synonym for kindness, honesty, and riches. Was there any name more vivid, direct, resonant, and full of meaning than this one for a website that would open up the gate to riches for ordinary people?

Jack Ma remained proud of this name for many years. In the beginning, however, he met with an unexpected problem when picking this name. Jack Ma decided to call the website he was going to found 'Alibaba' after much research and investigation. However, when he went to register it, he met with the message: "This domain name has already been registered."

To give up or go on? To start afresh or to seek out the person who set up the domain? Jack Ma chose the latter, for he felt that there was no other domain name which could express the spirit of his new website better than this one. He did some searching, and discovered that the web page had been registered by a Canadian. There was only one way to get the domain name and that was to buy it!

Jack Ma negotiated with the Canadian, who agreed to sell it for $10,000 US. Jack Ma did not hesitate. He used nearly one fifth of their start-up funds to make the purchase.

With this, the Chinese website Alibaba, headed by Jack Ma, was successfully registered online. Alibaba belonged to Jack Ma and his team. The head of Alibaba's marketing team, Zhang Pu, once elaborated on the meaning behind the domain name: "We felt that Alibaba was just great. Why?

"Firstly, because the story of Alibaba is an ancient Arabic legend that is famous all over the world.

"Secondly, Alibaba is very easy to spell, a crucial factor for domain names on the internet, which have to be easy for people to remember.

"Thirdly, it is rich in meaning. When people hear the name Alibaba, what is the first thing they think of? 'Open sesame!' Of course people will think of 'open sesame', because the story is about treasure and riches. Hence, basically everyone will think of 'open sesame' when they hear the name Alibaba.

"Alibaba is a platform aimed at serving businesses. Alibaba is perfect because it makes business owners think of making money. On another level, if people understand what the original story was about, they will know that the protagonist was an honest person who would never deceive others.

"This makes the name Alibaba very fitting for our company. We want to let everyone know that only honest businesses will be successful on the internet. This is the reason behind why we chose the domain name Alibaba."

Zhang Pu put it very well. Alibaba symbolized three things: wealth, honesty, and good luck. At that stage, the company was still not fully established, yet they were willing to spend one fifth of their start-up funds on a domain name. Not many people understood why Jack Ma did this, even including many of those closest to him. Yet Jack Ma persevered, for he believed it was worth every penny.

Jack Ma was proved right in 2006, when the Hurun Report on privately run businesses in China declared that the Alibaba brand was worth $2.7 billion US. Not long after, Jack Ma registered Alimama and Alibaobao, creating an entire Ali family – father, mother and baby. Following the domain name registration, the website and the company, Alibaba quietly set sail. It made sense for the launch to be quiet, for there was no great fanfare, no great advertising campaign or media endorsement. On the bank of West Lake, in Jack Ma's own home, 18 people started up their computers and connected to the internet, marking Alibaba's departure from port and the beginning of their new voyage.

There are some people who say with hindsight that this was another of Jack's business tactics. They say that by keeping the launch quiet, he was creating a sense of mystery that would attract the attention of the media and the public in a different way. Actually, this was not the case. The quiet launch was simply because they did not have enough money. At the beginning of June that year, the conglomerate 'giant' Alibaba had all but ex-hausted its funds. Its employees would only travel in inexpensive Xiali taxis – they did not dare get into any better cars. A dozen tired and worn-out figures slogged day and night at Jack Ma's house. They drank hot water when they were thirsty and ate instant noodles when they were hungry. When they felt tired, they would make up a little bed on the floor. With no advertising, not many people knew there was a company called Alibaba on the bank of West Lake. Their operations, however, were out of the ordinary.

Their aim was to create an international website. As they said themselves, they bypassed the amateur competitions and went straight for the World Cup. That is, they began by targeting foreign firms, many of which did not know where the website they were using was located.

After some time, America's *Business Weekly* came across the site and wanted to do an interview. They were unable to find where it was, so they set into motion all their investigative abilities. According to their analysis, they came to their conclusion that it was possibly in Hangzhou, China.

Business Weekly first contacted China's Ministry of Foreign Trade, then Zhejiang Province's Foreign Affairs Office. Finally, they ended up in Hangzhou. Their journalists got in contact with Jack Ma and found their headquarters on West Lake. When they knocked on the door and took a look inside, what they saw left them gobsmacked. Was this really Alibaba?

Alibaba already had several tens of thousands of clients at that point. They were located in the United States, Europe and Japan, and had quite an international reputation already. Despite the fact that their e-commerce platform was serving outstanding global businesses and well-known business figures, they were still working in the same room. The journalists were deeply moved by their working environment and sleeping spaces on the floor.

In May 1999, a famous media outlet in Hangzhou published a piece entitled, "Seeking to Engage in Global Trade, Alibaba Refuses Interview." How could a website that wanted to trade internationally refuse to do an interview? It was entirely unheard of. Why would a global trading website refuse the media's advances in an age when everyone was so desperate to be famous?

This question hung around in the minds of reporters and the mass media. It ignited their curiosity. Many journalists tried every possible means to get an audience with Alibaba. It was a great surprise for Jack Ma to find that his actions had produced such unexpected results.

Although he had done the opposite of trying to attract the media's attention, he seemed to have done just that. It was essentially a free media campaign. Sure enough, the influential *Business Weekly* produced a moving full-length report on Alibaba. The sense of mystery, coupled with the sudden appearance of the news article, made Alibaba famous around the world. The number of foreign hits and users of their website increased exponentially.

___

One of Jack Ma's statements about Alibaba does not seem to make sense. When he first set out, he said he wanted to build a company that would last 80 years. Later, he changed this number to 102. This figure leaves everyone in a kind of suspense, like an acrobatic trick designed to shock the audience. Is 100 not good enough? Is 110 not a nice number? Why is there a two on the end of the hundred?

Let us first take a look at the explanation he gave in 1980:

"A hundred seemed too much. Everyone talks about the figure 100, especially Chinese people. What's more, the average lifespan of a Chinese company is six to seven years. Hardly any make it to 13 years, let alone 18. Eighty years is therefore a monstrous target!

"Why does everyone have to live to 100 years old? I think 80 is more like a true life cycle. Everyone is conceived and born, they grow, they speed up, decline, and pass away. I think it is important for us to set a base of 80 years. We celebrated our fourth anniversary last week. Seventy-six years still lie ahead of us.

"If you ask me whether this company is successful or not, I will tell you that we must wait until 80 years in the future. If we perish before we reach that day, then we have not succeeded. If our dying day is after the 80-year mark, however, then we have won. I have never thought much about making large profits, for our company stands by four basic principles, the second of which is never to make making money our top priority."

"We want to change the lives of the businesses we serve. We want to create something of value for society and for our clients. This is our company's ultimate goal."

In addition to what he said then about his 80-year goal, Jack Ma gave a further explanation on a web forum of the city of Dongguan:

"Our original slogan in the year 2000 was to live for 80 years. We did not determine this figure randomly. We thought about it carefully. In 1999, many people in the internet industry ran away after their companies had been listed on the market for just eight months. Everyone in China said that you could loophole money on the internet. Then everyone ended up deserting. I am not concerned about how long you will wait to see. Only impatient people will get tired and leave when they hear 80 years."

This was how Jack Ma explained why he initially wanted to set up a company that would last for 80 years. If you read between the lines, you can see signs of his ambitious nature and sense of responsibility towards his clients. What did he mean by not wanting to make money? What was a company if it was not to make money?

In actual fact, this entrepreneur, who revered the hero Feng Qingyang in the Jin Yong novels, was talking sense. When he said that making money should not be their primary goal, what he meant was that it might be the second or the third. Indeed, the point of a business was to make money, but it should not be the first priority. Using undetectable methods to produce tangible results – that was Jack Ma's style.

What then, was Alibaba's first goal? To change the lives of the businesses they served and to create something of value for society and their clients. Once the society and client base that they were situated in possessed such value, then what they were trying to create could follow naturally. This was a much superior strategy to that of making money for its own sake. Following the latter method, you might be able to survive for one or two days, maybe even up to a few years. There would be no way for you to survive 80 years, however.

This is what made Jack's idea unique. It was the guiding principle behind Alibaba's survival methods and business operations. In 2004, Alibaba had made it to the five-year mark. It was during these celebrations that Jack Ma adjusted their goal and changed 80 years to 102. Given that it was born in the last year of the 20th century, then that would mean Alibaba's life would span three centuries, making it one of the greatest companies in China.

The dream you start with is very important in determining how far you will go eventually. Alibaba aimed to become a legendary international firm that would span three centuries from its founding in 1999, the last year of the 20th century, until 2101, the first year of the 22nd century. They could maximize their promise to guarantee clients' interests with long-lasting and stable development.

Jack Ma also said, "We want to create a great Chinese company. At the celebrations for Alibaba's tenth anniversary in 2009, we wanted to have entered the list of the top 500 companies worldwide.

"Your tactic is survival, so I want everyone to stop pursuing a success that they have not yet obtained. It is exactly when one feels they have succeeded that they begin to go downhill. We don't speak of failure. We do not accept success. We want to last for 102 years.

"Previously it was 80 years. Lots of people walked out when I said that figure. Now I want to make it 102. Now we want to make it to 100 years old, and two extra to make it into the next century. If I go bankrupt on 30 December of the year 2099, then I will still not claim success.

"Many companies look for opportunities to make money. I, on the other hand, research the organizing force behind enterprises that were set up over 100 years ago in order to reach my target of 102 years.

"The greatest difference between Alibaba and other companies is the force that gives us the power to establish an organization, a culture and a system. It is about the construction of a system with a financial department, an operations department and a team of implementers. It is the establishment of a system that stretches from the hiring of employees to their training, development and entire career.

"This is why we will not list overseas for a short-term advantage. Alibaba is only seven years old. We still have 95 years to go and a lot of fundamental skills that we must learn. I want to remain with my feet on the ground. I don't want [Alibaba] to become a huge international corporation while I stand at its head. I am simply not capable of that. Yet I firmly believe that my successors will be."

At the end of May 1999, when Alibaba was facing a funding crisis, a new figure came into Jack Ma's view. A delicate face, a pair of square-framed glasses, a stern mouth. He wore a sharp suit and leather shoes. Always poised and put-together, he gave off an air of resoluteness. Who was he?

His name was Cai Chongxin and he came with an impressive résumé. Born into a prestigious family in Taiwan, he was sent to America at the age of 13 to study. After that, he got into Yale University to study East Asian economics before going on to study for a PhD. In 1990, he successfully passed his law exams in New York to begin providing taxation law services. In 1994 he took up the position of vice-chairman and legal adviser at a New York foreign investment company which specialized in investment and acquisitions. In 1995, he became the vice-chairman and high-level investment manager of a subsidiary company in northern Europe that held the largest portion of shares in the industry. He oversaw the firm's Asian private equity investment fund.

It was obvious from his resumé that he was a well-educated and highly experienced investor. Moreover, his focus was on Asia, where Alibaba was situated.

Alibaba had a much greater reputation abroad than at home back then and on 10 March 1999, Alibaba launched an English-language website. This move attracted the attention of several authoritative international news media outlets including *Forbes* and *Newsweek*

Magazine. More and more people began to take an interest in this e-commerce website called Alibaba which had suddenly appeared.

It seemed almost fashionable to invest in internet companies at that time, which was when the internet was going through a period of rapid development. Alibaba was a rapidly developing site in the e-commerce sector. It was a youthful company full of energy, so it was very popular with many people.

Furthermore, e-commerce was coming into its prime period of development. As a result of this, Cai Chongxin paid a visit to Hangzhou in May 1999. His target was Jack Ma and Alibaba.

He and Jack Ma arranged to meet. It was a long discussion. Jack Ma did not think it anything special compared to other meetings he was having at the time. They were all a case of Jack Ma talking and the other person listening.

He spoke non-stop about e-commerce, about Alibaba, about his 80-year goal, his great idea, and becoming one of the top 500 global companies. Cai Chongxin interrupted him every so often, but the rest of the time it seemed he only needed a pair of ears, for his mouth had lost its function.

Then a feeling began to rise within him: trust, passion, ambition, and idealism, swirling in a wave of heat that began in the pit of Cai Chongxin's stomach and gradually began to throb through his limbs and eventually into every corner of his body. He found himself carried along and absorbed by it.

This was not imaginary, it was real. Jack Ma's talent for delivering speeches, combined with the bright prospects of Alibaba and Cai Chongxin's background in international investment, together with his understanding of the internet industry and Alibaba, made for an exciting prospect.

It ought to be said that the primary factor that grabbed his attention was Jack Ma's gift for speaking. Second was the boundless prospects of the e-commerce industry, and last came his own insight and intellect.

Someone once made a vivid comparison: that a chick will hatch from its egg when exposed to warmth, but a stone will remain a mere stone whatever the temperature. Cai Chongxin had business experience in many countries all over the world. He was well educated, daring, and resourceful. He was an experienced investor and international businessman. He would not make a leap of faith just based on a simple conversation.

He found Jack Ma, though short in stature, to be a natural business leader. He had a charm about him that could lead a team to achieve the lofty targets he had announced. Cai Chongxin said with a wave of his hand, "How about this, Jack Ma: why don't you take me to have a look around your company?"

Jack Ma hesitated momentarily. Company? His company was still as humble as ever. Hiding was no use, though, for Cai Chongxin was giving him a stern glare.

Jack Ma had no choice but to take Cai Chongxin for a tour around his house by the West Lake. Chongxin leapt back in surprise as soon as he opened the door.

The so-called 18 Arhats were full of vigour, despite their 24-hour schedules, beds on the floor, and diet of instant noodles and plain water. In this basic room, they served millions of clients all over the world, creating the best business opportunities for them and later becoming one of the top 500 companies in the world.

Cai Chongxin turned to look at Jack Ma. The little man who had boasted so shamelessly showed no sign of regret. Rather, he even stretched out a hand and said: "Please, Mr Cai, this is our Ali company headquarters."

Chongxin was both a businessman and a scholar. He not only understood the way business worked, but also viewed life like a philosopher. In that instant, he was struck by the roomful of workaholics who refused to admit when they were exhausted. After some discussions, he found the staff there to be full of confidence and enthusiasm for what they were doing. If there was such a thing as a madman, then he had found a whole group of them.

They believed in the 80-year promise and in reaching the global top 500 companies. They believed in Jack Ma, that this short man would bring them a bright future. Cai Chongxin stayed there for a long time inspecting their facilities. His stern exterior continued to be turned upside down by the heatwave ignited by Jack Ma's words, making it difficult for him to calm down for a long time.

Perhaps he saw a pursuit of idealism in Jack Ma. At the Alibaba headquarters, he saw a firm foundation, trust, and a clear picture of what tomorrow would hold.

Chongxin did not say anything at that point. He just gave Jack Ma a very firm handshake and said, "See you again!" Jack Ma could not help but be taken aback for, after all, Chongxin was an executive who had come to Hangzhou to make investments. Yet all he had said was "See you again", with no talk of investment at all.

Jack Ma was a rather resourceful individual, so he was not about to let this big fish slip out of his net. He hastily followed up with the question, "Mr Cai, sir, what about your investment programme?"

"I am going to return to Hong Kong to report back to our headquarters. Let's discuss things further next time." Cai Chongxin left Jack Ma with a little shred of hope before leaving on a direct flight back to Hong Kong.

Two weeks later, he was back. He did not break his promise. Furthermore, Jack's eyes lit up when he saw a beautiful woman standing by Chongxin's side. Cai Chongxin gave a casual introduction: "This is the head of the Alibaba Corporation and the manager of a future global top 500 company, Jack Ma. This is my wife."

Jack Ma was naturally very welcoming. In June 1999, Alibaba had already spent every penny of its 500,000 yuan start-up fund. Where would next month's wages come from? Jack Ma and his staff were uncertain. It was Chongxin who turned out to be their saviour.

Jack Ma was shrewd enough to realize that, since Cai Chongxin had come to Hangzhou twice, there was still a chance that he would choose to invest. Otherwise, he had no reason to visit Hangzhou or Jack Ma a second time.

He told himself, "Keep calm." The other party had already shown that he was interested, so what need was there for Jack Ma to come across as desperate? It would be best for him to maintain an air of indifference: "I might not even be interested whether you want to invest or not!"

Only in this manner could Jack Ma guarantee that the investor would not impose too many strict terms in the contract. Jack Ma had an astute business mind, so this was naturally his first reaction. He was well versed in this key principle of discussing business.

However, Cai Chongxin still did not mention anything relating to investment. They seemed to be locked in a wrestling match. Neither of them was willing to mention the matter, prolonging the process greatly. It seemed that official matters were no longer very important and their daily itineraries were filled with activities more suited to two friends than two business partners.

It seemed that they had exchanged roles this time. Cai Chongxin spoke more than Jack Ma, who was busy anticipating the point when Chongxin would finally make a proposal, for it was the investor who needed to know more about the other party. This was the only way he could avoid losing capital and maximize his profit.

Yet Cai Chongxin seemed to want to talk about anything but investing. The most he was willing to ask was about Jack's friends and family. He raised topics such as the Summer Palace in Beijing and that line from the famous Song Dynasty poem about the Jiangsu region by the poet Wang Anshi: "The spring wind breathes green onto the banks of the Yangtze River." These were all quite personal topics of conversation, and rather far removed from official business.

Jack Ma answered his questions without really thinking about his answers. He was still anxious to know when Cai Chongxin would turn to the matter of investment. They were like two expert t'ai chi boxers, circling one another, neither willing to strike first.

One day, Jack Ma finally decided that he could not bear it any longer. He wanted to lay his cards on the table. He invited Cai Chongxin and his wife to take a boat out on West Lake. It was a warm and sunny day. West Lake was as beautiful as ever, like a beautiful woman full of grace and feeling. Shy, yet cordial, she welcomed them.

They neared the centre of the lake. In the distance, the pavilions were shrouded in a delicate mist. Nearby on the Su Causeway, a famous landmark of the Northern Song Dynasty, the willows danced gracefully. Sitting in the stern of the boat, Jack Ma felt that the time was right. He could wait no longer, and neither did he want to. As soon as he opened his mouth, he was going to raise the question that had been bouncing around in his head for so long. Suddenly he realized that Chongxin, who was sitting in front of him, had thrown down his oar and turned round to speak to him: "I am quitting my position in Hong Kong. I want to join Alibaba and work alongside you. What do you think?"

There was no breeze. The lake surface was completely calm. West Lake lay like a maiden holding her breath beneath them. In the distance, a pair of purple swallows flitted across the water, creating a line of ripples.

Jack Ma looked at Chongxin intently, but his expression was completely serious and he showed no sign that he was joking. His wife was nodding at Jack Ma, as if to say, "Really!"

Jack Ma leapt to his feet, causing the boat to rock from side to side in a rather alarming manner, which reminded him that he was not on land, so he hastily sat back down. "Mr Cai! You're not kidding me, are you? I can't afford to employ you! You earn a six-figure salary in Hong Kong. Here, you will only get 500 yuan a month!"

Up until then, Chongxin's wife had not said anything, but at that point she interrupted, saying, "If you don't allow him to join you now, you may regret it for the rest of your life."

Chongxin said, "That's right. I've even brought my wife with me here. If that doesn't mean that I want to stay, then I don't know what does! Please do take me in!" Jack Ma scanned their faces again. He realized that Chongxin's decision was the result of careful deliberation and had already been approved by his wife. It looked as if Chongxin had made up his mind.

Jack Ma thought for a moment, then replied, "Alright then. Seeing as you're already set on the move, then you might as well join us! You can start by helping us look after our finances. It just so happens that we need someone with your expert knowledge of both law and economics."

It later proved that it had been crucial for Cai Chongxin to join Alibaba at that time. Its importance was incalculable. Time also proved that Cai Chongxin really did deserve to be called the cream of the crop in the business world. With just one glance, he had recognized the potential of Jack Ma and his team, and the boundless possibilities for the future of Alibaba. Otherwise, he certainly would not have given up the excellent situation he had in Hong Kong to join a company whose employees slept on the floor.

Jack Ma had his charm, his team had their infectious enthusiasm, and Cai Chongxin had his discerning eye. The conversation on the little boat on West Lake seemed to have decided many matters, but at the end of the day it most clearly proved the three points mentioned above. Chongxin returned to his headquarters in Hong Kong immediately afterwards to tender his resignation.

When Cai Chongxin joined Alibaba, the backers, investors, and shareholders did not even have a written agreement. That meant that this company, which was looking to do business for at least 80 years, had still no clear shareholding arrangement. It completely lacked awareness of what having stocks entailed, let alone any clear concept of where the dividing line lay between the associated power and responsibility.

To put it bluntly, they were nothing more than an aimless herd of sheep on the battlefield of the business world, even including their head, Jack Ma.

Cai Chongxin entered the headquarters of Alibaba, and became one of the herd. Of course, Jack Ma had given him a very important task, to oversee the company's overall financial affairs and act as their consultant for legal affairs.

Jack Ma had an eye for other people's talent and knew how to make best use of it. Cai Chongxin had a talent for business management and for discerning other people's characters. He had more experience in the managing and running of international ventures. Hence, they hit it off from the start.

They started out by reorganizing the company structure of Alibaba. There is no doubt that this was of chief importance in building an international corporation. Lofty ideals had to be combined with a practical management structure, in line with international protocol.

However, Cai Chongxin was surprised to discover that the 18 founders of the company did not have even one contract agreement between them. It seemed Chongxin had arrived at just the right time. Jack Ma said to him jokingly: "We have not officially become a company yet because we were waiting for you to come and set it up for us."

Chongxin himself drafted an equity participation contract, rather beautifully written in English. It was completely watertight, and fully complied with international regulations. It was the standard requirement for an international company.

Chongxin sent a copy of the contract to each of the shareholders, but they could not understand it. Hence, Chongxin patiently explained it to everyone in Jack Ma's home. It was over 30 degrees at that time and there was no air-conditioning, only an old electric fan. Chongxin was accustomed to wearing a suit and leather shoes, rendering him rather overheated. He had no choice but to remove his jacket, only to find that his shirt had been utterly soaked through with sweat.

He did not only speak of the contract. He started right from the beginning with the subject of the structure of equity shares, shareholders' rights, and the dilution of shares. This was a lesson on the organization of international business. It was not only compulsory listening for the 18 followers and Jack Ma, but could also be seen as making up for many previously missed lessons. If they did not make up for lost time now, then their company would never grow beyond the stage of a young seedling.

Jack Ma and and his team were won over by Cai Chongxin. He really was one of those classic Chinese people who have been to study and work abroad before returning home. He was a true scholar and a highly experienced director of international investments. He was dedicated to his work and willing to instruct them for hours on end. They would have been willing to follow him out onto any battlefield. They learned a lot from his lessons. Of course, they still had quite a few unanswered questions, but as long as Mr Cai was there, they would grasp the concept of what 'international' and 'big corporation' meant in no time.

Jack Ma took the initiative to be the first to sign his name on the contract. When the others saw their leader put his name down, they too picked up their pens, half understanding and half not. It was a vitally important process, for it signified that the stockholding position of the founders of Alibaba had finally been stipulated fully in law, and laid the foundation for when they would make their fortunes eight years on.

Not long afterwards, they received a large amount of funding from an international investor, thanks to the addition of Cai Chongxin to their team. In total it came to 5 million dollars.

It is scarcely necessary to repeat what it meant for Cai Chongxin to join the company. After receiving such substantial funds, Jack Ma, who had never been lacking in ambition or bravery, set his sights on Hong Kong. Although it had declined slightly as an international financial and trade centre in recent years, it had still retained its position as a key trade capital. It would open a door to the rest of the world for Alibaba if they could extend their reach there.

Cai Chongxin was now chief financial officer (CFO). Jack Ma said to him, "Mr Cai, we're going to Hong Kong, a place you are very familiar with. Only you can set up our headquarters there. Now you are to be the CEO of the Alibaba headquarters in Hong Kong." Hence, Chongxin wasted no time in heading straight for the city whose name means 'Fragrant Port'.

Cai Chongxin later said this about the matter: "The people who work here tend to do something I find rather interesting. According to them, when making important life decisions, you should rely more on the strong feeling in your gut than on reason. I like working with people who have passion and zeal. I like taking risks! So I decided to join here. That's all it was."

CHAPTER

HOISTING THE SAILS

There is another person who must be discussed alongside Alibaba, and that is Masayoshi Son. Strictly speaking, he was a Japanese-born Korean; that is to say, he was Japanese with Korean heritage. Yet, speaking even more strictly, his ancestors were Chinese. He had retained the surname Son – a Japanese form of the Chinese family name Sun – because of his Chinese heritage. He was not a tall man either, roughly the same height as Jack Ma, or perhaps a little bit taller. However, his forehead was huge, almost like that of the film actor Ge You. A large forehead is considered a sign of intelligence. According to Ge You, "No hair sprouts above an astute brain."

Masayoshi Son, however, was not only intelligent; just like Jack Ma, he possessed great wisdom. At that time, he was the richest individual in Asia.

Jack Ma and Alibaba had gained the recognition of the investment bank Goldman Sachs, thanks to the fact that Cai Chongxin had joined the firm. The first sum of 5 million dollars had already been advanced. However, the internet was developing more rapidly by the day. Alibaba needed to adapt to the global situation and make swift progress. Funding was still the principal prerequisite.

In California's Silicon Valley, Jack Ma met with the managers of more than 40 investment banks, yet not a single one of them displayed any interest in e-commerce. Not one of them realized that Alibaba would become a huge international corporation. This meant that not one of the investment bank managers was interested in investing in the Chinese company.

Jack Ma was rather irritated by this fact. From Silicon

Valley to San Francisco, he had witnessed nothing but prosperity and bustle. Even at night, the roads there were rivers of light. The flow of traffic never slowed. Industrious Americans pursued global trends day and night, doing all they could to make their dreams into reality.

Jack Ma promised himself in that moment that he would make Alibaba big and successful. A Chinese company had to make it into the top 500. They needed to be as industrious as the Americans he had seen, and reach for the stars!

Yet his funding bottleneck was restricting the company's development. It was just when he was worrying about this matter that an Indian friend of his recommended Masayoshi Son.

His Indian friend was called Guta and was a highly experienced analyst. He sent Jack Ma an email saying, "There is someone who would like to meet with you. The person in question will certainly be of use to you." Jack Ma immediately flew to Beijing where Masayoshi Son was staying.

There were many experts from the internet industry gathered that day at the Fuhua Mansion. Dressed in a rather ordinary jacket, Jack Ma entered the room with half a sheet of paper in his hand.

There was a screen in the room onto which was projected the home page of Alibaba's website. Masayoshi Son swept his gaze over the screen before saying, "You have 20 minutes to speak." Yet after Jack Ma had spoken for just six minutes, Masayoshi Son waved his hand and shouted, "Stop!"

Then he asked directly, "How much investment do you need?"

He did not expect this short and scrawny little man in a worn-out jacket would actually have the gall to say, "I received the funds I needed yesterday. I do not need any more."

Masayoshi Son was stunned. He asked: "If you don't need any more funds, then why have you sought me out?"

Jack Ma replied, rather obstinately, "I didn't come of my own accord. It was a friend who asked me to."

Just like that, things took a turn in the opposite direction once again. Masayoshi Son immediately decided that SoftBank, the Japanese multinational internet corporation which he had founded, would invest 30 million US dollars in Alibaba. Jack Ma later decided that this would be too much, so he reduced the sum by 10 million, leaving Masayoshi Son's overall investment at 20 million.

Many years later, they met again. Jack Ma said to Masayoshi Son: "People often say that you are quite crazy. I'm pretty crazy too. I have a question. Why did you decide to invest 100 million US dollars in a tiny company like Yahoo 15 years ago? Why did it take you only six minutes to decide to invest 20 million in Alibaba when the internet industry was going through a drought nine years ago?"

Masayoshi Son said: "I believed in Jerry Yang. I discovered him. I saw passion and ability in his eyes, and so I decided to invest 100 million US dollars when Yahoo had just been founded in order to expedite their path to international success.

"Similarly, when I saw you nine years ago, you had nothing to your name, and the internet industry in China had only just started out. However, you had a pair of glistening eyes that revealed your dreams and your enthusiasm. I felt that you were just as crazy as Jerry Yang, so I decided to invest in your company. We are both 'madmen'. There is one thing that is different, though. You are still as thin as you were all those years ago, yet I seem to have gotten a little heavier."

Jack Ma replied: "I understand. It seems that a little bit of craziness is the key to success. You need big dreams, passion and a good strategy."

Masayoshi Son said, "That's right. In the first six minutes I saw you, I felt that you were very genuine. At the time, I believed Alibaba was going to become as big as Google. Google developed on account of its advertising. Alibaba not only had advertising to rely on, but also personal connections. This meant that Alibaba had a better chance at stability.

"China was going to become the country with the largest GDP in the world, and Alibaba had access to a global market, not just China. That's why I hoped that I could expand my success with you and your company."

Jack Ma asked, "Alibaba was still quite small-scale at the time. What made you so confident?"

Masayoshi Son replied: "I said when I saw you, yours will become the first true Chinese internet company which implements a business model invented by Chinese people themselves and that becomes the world number one based on exactly this model. Back then, the success of many internet companies, no matter whether they were Japanese or European, was just based on copying the American model.

"Alibaba invented a new business model, so you had to succeed. I felt that Alibaba was a great company. When I met you, I said that you were a hero, that one day people would compare you to Jerry Yang and Bill Gates, because all of you were responsible for creating a totally new model."

This was the conversation that Masayoshi Son and Jack Ma had nine years later, and a prime example of two great men appreciating one another. In 2003, Masayoshi Son called to invite Jack Ma to Tokyo. They did not discuss financial particulars, but rather sat and swapped ideas about major trends in the internet industry.

Just before they were going to sign their names on the new contract, they went to the bathroom to relieve themselves. In the bathroom, Jack Ma put forward a figure of 82 million US dollars. Masayoshi Son agreed without hesitating, and shortly after they signed the agreement on the conference table with no hitches at all. With this, Alibaba entered the C2C (customer to customer) market and Taobao Marketplace was born. C2C businesses are facilitators that enable their clients to deal directly with one another. Later on, China Yahoo was annexed by Alibaba, and Yahoo China bought a 40% share in Alibaba's stocks with 1 billion US dollars in cash, as well as Yahoo China's services. Being the largest shareholder in Yahoo China, Masayoshi Son joined forces with Alibaba once again. Jack Ma was made a board member of SoftBank.

The two men were becoming increasingly close in the e-commerce and internet spheres. They very much admired one another, but did not give in to one another's interest in the matter of profit. Sometimes their views were at odds when it came to specific questions such as the purchase of Yahoo China and the transfer of Alibaba's online payment platform Alipay. As neither of them were fond of compromise, there were often disputes.

Perhaps this is what business and joint shares mean. At the end of the day, Jack Ma was a visionary and Masayoshi Son had great foresight. The very day that he invested in Alibaba, he started making an exponential return. Jack Ma would not lose to Masayoshi Son, and Masayoshi Son was definitely worthy of him.

———

It was in 2003 that Taobao was born. Not long after, Alipay was launched following its development by Jack Ma and his team. Taobao was a roaring success, which contributed to the rapid development of Alibaba's e-commerce sector. However, competition was never far away in the business world.

They met head on with EachNet. At the time, EachNet held the greatest share in the individual transaction e-commerce market in China. Headed by a board of directors and CGO, Shao Yibo, it already had its feet firmly on the ground. It seemed impossible for Taobao to overtake it.

Shao Yibo was 26 years old and had been a mathematical prodigy ever since he was young. He had graduated from Harvard University. He was exceedingly knowledgeable and full of vigour. Under his leadership, EachNet advanced with bloodthirsty battle cries, ready to meet Taobao head on.

As a result, you could see adverts for both companies in many cities, at subway station entrances, public transport stops, and newspaper stands. EachNet had 3.5 million registered users back then. There was a new product uploaded every second, a new bid every ten seconds, and a completed transaction every minute. In total, there were 2,350,000 products on the site, and it had amassed 800 million yuan's worth of transactions.

This was how formidable EachNet was. In 2003, it joined forces with the world's largest internet commerce company, eBay. eBay gave 150 million US dollars in funding and bought 67% of EachNet's stocks, becoming the largest shareholder behind the scenes at EachNet. EachNet had formidable operating experience, bountiful funds, and the support of a global corporation.

Yet Jack Ma was born brave. On 7 July 2003, he announced publicly, "Alibaba will invest 100 million yuan in setting up the website Taobao which will offer a platform for both B2C [business to consumer] and C2C transactions."

"Crazy Jack Ma has gone crazy once again!" This was the most popular headline used by the media at the time. There was a very influential article written which claimed that, "Jack Ma has irrationally wasted 100,000,000 yuan and ruined Taobao's reputation." The article asked: "Is Jack Ma's behaviour rational when the e-commerce marketplace is still so uncertain in China? ... The waters of the e-commerce sector are deep and murky. Will people really be able to find any treasures on Taobao? Only time will tell." (*Taobao* is Chinese for 'panning for treasures'.)

The media's doubt was understandable. At that time, internet industries were going through a severe drought, with no sign of rain. Jack Ma was about to make the biggest investment ever made in the internet industry. Moreover, EachNet already held 80% of the market share and was managed by the experienced American company eBay.

Jack Ma's opponent was no longer just the young Shao Yibo. Now he was faced with the veteran CEO Meg Whitman, a heavyweight boxing champion compared to small, skinny Jack Ma.

How was the battle going to be fought? Perhaps the winners and the losers had already been decided. Regardless, the stage curtains quietly opened on the act. Quietly, because Meg Whitman did not even acknowledge her opponent Jack Ma. From her elevated position she saw only what was in front of her, and completely overlooked him. Perhaps this was one of the reasons EachNet failed. When Taobao first set out, EachNet never paid any attention to it, and definitely never expected to compete with it.

In addition, Meg Whitman seems to have overlooked the fact that Jack Ma had a formidable backer behind him. That backer was Masayoshi Son, who decided to invest another 82 million US dollars in Alibaba, with the specific aim of setting up a B2C platform.

Jack Ma was just like the Monkey King of Chinese

legend with his transfiguration powers. As soon as he heard the word 'grow', he could enlarge to stand as tall as the sky. The giant Meg Whitman was stunned when she met with Jack Ma after he had taken on this sudden growth spurt, leaving her with no time to react.

Yet Meg Whitman, after all, deserved her reputation as an archetypal businesswoman, and a world-class one at that. eBay had already taken over the C2C markets in America, Germany, the UK, Canada, France, Korea, and Australia by that time. China was her next big target. This was because the Chinese market was still developing rapidly. The number of computer and internet users was surging. There was no limit to the development of e-commerce in China.

Whitman told the investors and analysts of Wall Street that eBay was going to win China without a doubt. Only when eBay had control of the Chinese market could the company fill in the final missing pieces of its global territorial puzzle. Her stance when it came to EachNet was, "Give whatever and however much it takes."

Meanwhile, Jack Ma was already very clear about what Whitman's final goal was. He believed that she was ultimately going to set up an e-commerce platform that would break down the barriers between B2B and C2C platforms. If he did not make a move now, then Alibaba would run the risk of being completely wiped out.

There is no compromise in war. There is only 'You die and I live'. Little Jack Ma was aware of this principle, and the successful career woman, Whitman, was even more so. They went into battle with their rifles ready loaded.

In July 2003, Whitman made this announcement after acquiring a controlling number of shares in EachNet: "Within the next eighteen months, the battle for the Chinese e-commerce market will be over."

Jack Ma objected to this statement. He took no notice of the unwritten rules followed by Western businesses. He had faith in the Chinese saying that "Even the strongest dragon cannot hold down a local snake." He said that "Foreign companies do not understand China."

The campaign started with EachNet investing in the search engines Google and Baidu (a Chinese web company whose many services include an online encyclopedia resembling Wikipedia). An advert appeared on Taobao's website that said: "If you're looking for treasure, head to EachNet!" On EachNet's homepage, a banner read "Open a shop and pan for treasures – enjoy life to the fullest" – a clear breach of Taobao's copyright. Jack Ma submitted a complaint immediately. EachNet was reprimanded and forced to take down the ads. However, Whitman was an astute and experienced businesswoman. She decided to concentrate on increasing site traffic – more site traffic meant more customers. In July 2003, when the newborn Taobao went to advertise its site, it suddenly found that every web portal was already covered in adverts for eBay. Even if Taobao had the funds, there was no way they could compete. No one would pay attention.

It turned out that Whitman had paid more than the going rate for an advert. Aside from advertising EachNet, she also wanted to block out adverts for rival websites such as Taobao, Aupo, Ebid, Artrade and Yahoo Auction.

The agreement that EachNet had signed with many web portals clearly stated that if they conducted marketing for any websites belonging to Taobao and related companies, there would be a heavy penalty.

Advertising was the basis of making business transactions. In short, without advertising there was no business. Jack Ma found he had been blocked on all sides by Whitman, forcing him to implement a rather indirect breakthrough strategy.

Almost overnight, adverts for Taobao appeared on thousands of personal websites. They also circulated across underground stations and on public buses.

In response to the adverts of the two companies, one commentator pointed out: "If the site traffic of four major web portals is around 800,000 per day, then that is the audience that EachNet's adverts are reaching. Taobao, on the other hand, has been driven onto small- to medium-scale websites.

"That being given, China has several million small- to medium-scale websites. Even if the site traffic of each one is only 10,000 people, Taobao can still easily reach the same numbers as EachNet. What's more, it's obvious that they ask for a much lower price than the major web portals.

"The results of these two advertising techniques are also quite different. Everyone knows that although we visit major sites to check things like the news on a daily basis, the majority of our time is still spent on small- to medium-scale sites and forums. This means that it is actually more effective to go small-scale when it comes to advertising."

Of course, Jack Ma had still not given up on the role that the mainstream media could play. On 5 April 2004, Taobao officially announced in Guangzhou that they were going into partnership with the media outlet 21CN. Both parties would be implementing comprehensive cooperation in areas such as television, text messaging platforms, email sites, and marketing events. 21CN was a subsidiary company of China Telecom. It was the largest internet portal in the south of China and one of the top ten largest portals nationwide.

Jack Ma had set a precedent in Guangzhou, and just eight days later, on 13 April, both Sina and Yahoo announced the launch of the online inventory 1PAI.com, which was also of use to Taobao.

With the rise of yet another opponent, Whitman's blocking techniques were bound to fail after taking a beating from all sides. At that time, Taobao was not only remaining calm and collected in market terms when it came to EachNet. The company was also gathering its strength as far as its basic infrastructure was concerned. Jack Ma decided to sell Alipay in order to resolve the issue of accountability when it came to C2C transactions and remove conflicts of interest.

Alipay swiftly increased Taobao's reputation for trustworthiness after going into partnership with the Industrial and Commercial Bank of China to provide online payment and with the Identity Card Inspection Centre of the Ministry of Public Security. Customers began to flock to Taobao.

At the same time, Taobao launched an instant chat

tool called Taobao Wangwang which allowed customers to contact the seller directly when making a purchase. The instant chat tool replaced other software alternatives such as QQ. Although Wangwang was certainly not as big as QQ, it was more purposefully designed. It was created precisely for online transactions, so many of its functions were a product of and an aid to online communication between buyers and sellers.

Wangwang was also more innovative than QQ. It may have been a copy, but it was a creative one, designed with practical requirements in mind. Its launch gained widespread approval, for it really did meet members' individual requirements. Although it still only provided a communication platform, netizens felt that it managed to fulfil their particular needs when it came to online transactions.

The arrival of Wangwang meant the first subdivision of the Chinese instant chat market. It avoided going into direct competition with QQ, and was considered a greater breakthrough in terms of a business model. From a business perspective, its features, design, target users and actual usability all conformed to the particularities of online transactions.

This was very important. Alipay and Taobao Wangwang were two great props holding Taobao firmly up during its struggle against EachNet. Faced with the rapid advances that Taobao was making, eBay began to consider what countertactics it could take. It needed to change in order to attract more internet users to join EachNet and prevent Taobao's plans for expansion from succeeding.

On 13 June, EachNet publicly announced that it was going to cancel its plans for placing limits on sellers. This move did not only fail to gain popularity, but it actually damaged sellers in quite a big way. According to statistics published by Taobao, its website had 500,000 online users that day, a figure so large that it sometimes caused their servers to crash.

What was interesting was that the media did not add any fuel to the fire during this business battle. EachNet and Taobao were having a showdown. The cutting-edge newcomer Taobao resisted being gobbled up by the veteran EachNet. Many articles appeared in the newspapers announcing that Taobao had taken the lead when it came to e-commerce. Simultaneously, international media began to pay attention to this battle for the C2C market.

Reuters news agency quoted the market research analysts Piper Jaffray, saying, "In the next five years, everyone's gaze will be fixed on China. The competition here is fierce, and is only in its infancy. eBay will not necessarily become the market leader." Reuters themselves published an article which pointed out that Taobao had already become a formidable opponent for eBay.

Of course, Reuters was speaking from an Anglo-American perspective. An online article published by a Singaporean retailer pointed out that "Taobao has already become the number one website for C2C e-commerce in China."

According to the sample survey undertaken by the reporters, 70% of the individual sellers on eBay China had also chosen to sell through Taobao's platform.

EachNet, which had tight control of more than 50% of China's C2C market in 2003, had not expected to be pulled out of its saddle by Taobao just a year on. Meg Whitman was obviously quite startled to see that Taobao was now the front-runner!

Jack Ma became more daring as the battle went on. On 19 July, Alibaba announced that it was going to invest 350 million yuan in its subsidiary Taobao. This was in addition to the 100 million yuan that had been invested a year previously. In total, Alibaba had invested 540 million yuan in Taobao.

In September 2004, statistics revealed that the number of individual users on Taobao was approximately three times the amount on EachNet. On 21 September, Taobao published their transaction data. The total for August was 120 million yuan, and the average daily figures for September had already reached 7 million. The performance figures for the second quarter of 2004 published by eBay–EachNet, on the other hand, show that their total monthly transactions were 160 million yuan.

Consider the difference between the number of users of each site. There were 6,090,000 new users on EachNet, and 2,020,000 on Taobao. This meant that the number of completed individual user transactions on Taobao was more than three times that of EachNet.

On 20 October 2005, Jack Ma announced that he was going to increase investment into Taobao by one billion yuan. He said that eBay was trying to establish a global platform in China, and this was just like "trying to drive a first-class motor along a small dirt track". He also stated that eBay's leadership was very good at leading group combat, but they had no knowledge of guerrilla tactics.

Jack Ma compared Alibaba to a crocodile in the Yangtze River. Or, to put it another way: "We are fighting with a seawater shark. If we enter the ocean we will die, there is no doubt about that. Yet if we stay in the Yangtze River, we have a chance of winning."

In October 2006, Meg Whitman announced that she was going to sell eBay – EachNet. On 20 December 2006, eBay–EachNet went into partnership with the Chinese mobile internet company TOM Online; eBay–EachNet China and 40 million US dollars were used to acquire 49% of the shares. TOM Online bought 51% of the shares with its local management experience and 20 million US dollars.

After the agreement was made, the joint company name became TOM–EachNet. Wang Leilei was appointed as CEO.

At the same time, Wang Leilei stated "We cannot compete with an opponent which can afford to not even calculate its costs." Jack Ma's position was that he hoped to work with eBay.

The battle was finally over, and not a single gunshot had been fired. Jack Ma was the victor. Taobao was the declared leader of the Chinese C2C market.

CHAPTER

TRIALS
AND
TRIBULATIONS

On 10 December 2002, Huang Xingchu, the chef of a restaurant in the Luohu District of Shenzhen, came down with a fever. As a result, China and the rest of the world became aware of an infectious disease named Severe Acute Respiratory Syndrome (SARS). It was highly infectious and deadly, putting every single person at risk.

It came like a storm, ruthlessly sweeping through every corner of the globe, its epicentre spiralling out from China. Jack Ma and his colleagues became immediately aware of the fact that during the SARS epidemic, people would rather shop online.

SARS might be rampant, but life had to go on.

By March 2003, the prediction made by the people at Alibaba had become reality: there were 3,500 new members every day. This figure was 50% higher than that of the previous quarter. Existing members also strengthened the overall online transaction rate.

According to statistics, there were 900 to 1,200 new business opportunities posted every day. This was three times higher than at the same time the previous year. The amount of feedback given by international buyers doubled compared to the previous quarter. There was a four-fold increase in the number of times international buyers searched for the top 30 most popular products in China, and the number of suppliers doubled compared to the same time the previous year.

Every month, the website had 185 million hits and 2.4 million instances of transactions, enquiries, and feedback; 380,000 buyers and 1.9 million sellers from all over the globe sought out business opportunities and conducted all kinds of transactions through Alibaba.

On 30 April, by which time SARS had reached its peak, the major of Hangzhou, Mao Linsheng, came to Alibaba's headquarters for a one-hour fact-finding visit. He hoped, in these exceptional circumstances, that the e-commerce industry could invigorate local trade and help businesses break free from their current plight.

Many people felt at the time that doing business online was the most feasible and risk-free strategy for small- to medium-scale businesses. In the eyes of Alibaba, which had made such businesses its primary target, this was a heaven-sent opportunity.

Yet there are always two sides to everything. Just as Alibaba's business was starting to take off, a mishap occurred. On 11 April, a 26-year-old employee of Alibaba flew to Guangzhou to take part in the China Export Commodities Fair. She stayed a full seven days in this SARS disaster zone.

People were incredulous. They demanded, rather outraged: "How could people not know that there had been an outbreak of SARS? Why did they send staff on a business trip there, then of all times?"

Alibaba's explanation was: "This was the first time we attended the China Export Commodities Fair, and we met with SARS. Although many people are staying away from crowded places, we had already promised our clients that we would attend the fair. Alibaba had to go, whatever the circumstances."

Despite the fact that Guangzhou had already declared itself a red-alert zone for SARS, the fair was imminent and Alibaba could not break its promise to clientele.

In those seven days, the Alibaba representative was exceptionally busy. On the afternoon of 18 April, she flew back to Hangzhou. On the 21st, she still went in to work despite having been worked off her feet. Yet on the 22nd, she came down with symptoms such as a blocked nose, a sore throat, and phlegm. She consulted a hospital doctor who prescribed medication, but she did not see any improvement after taking it, so two days later she decided to stop using it.

From 28 to 30 April, she decided to go in to work despite not having fully recovered. On 2 May, she was overcome with a fever. On the 3rd, she went back to the hospital for examination. By the 5th, she had a temperature of 39°C (102°F).

At 6 o'clock in the evening at the hospital, specialists from Zhejiang's and Hangzhou's SARS teams diagnosed her as a "possible SARS case". On the evening of the 7th, she was transferred to the SARS clinic to confirm the diagnosis.

It all happened so quickly, everyone was in shock. People turned pale at the very mention of this highly infectious disease that seemed to be everywhere at once. It seemed to pace like a ghost around Alibaba headquarters, quickly scattering everyone in sight.

This was the fourth case in Hangzhou. The city government ordered Alibaba's headquarters to be quarantined. It became an isolated area within the city. In response, Jack Ma sent a letter to his staff saying: "Dear Ali friends, I have been rather heavy-hearted these past few days! I have been desperate to express my sincere apologies to you all ever since I learned the diagnosis had been confirmed this morning.

"If there was anything that could be exchanged for the recovery of our colleague who has unfortunately contracted the disease, or to guarantee the health of our other staff and the rest of the population of Hangzhou, I would be willing to give everything I have! It's true, there are still many aspects of Alibaba which are lacking. There are many questions that we must reflect on after the disaster has passed.

"As the person in charge of the company, I am willing to take full responsibility for what has happened, if I can. Yet reasoning tells me that today is not the time to start blaming others. Today, I need everyone to pull together to make it through this crisis and meet the challenges facing us head on. We are a young company formed by young people. Getting through this [crisis] will make us grow up very quickly. Let us join together in prayer for our colleague who has fallen ill, and wish her a speedy recovery!"

At 4 o'clock in the afternoon of 6 May, Jack Ma, wearing a face mask, made an announcement to everybody. A message was sent out simultaneously to everyone working at home. Everyone put masks on. They hurried to gather everything they would need at home. In just two hours, technical engineers had installed all the necessary software on their computers.

The most important thing for the Alibaba staff returning home was to isolate themselves. They locked their doors, and gave the keys to the guard at the front gate of their compounds. There were stations for epidemic prevention and officials from the Ministry of Public Security outside.

Breakfast, lunch and dinner were delivered to their compounds on a daily basis. Every day, someone wearing a thick hazard suit would visit every household with a large canister on their back and a long hose, which they used to spray every room while families kept clear. Just like a pesticide specialist, they sprayed the home then left.

This was a huge blow for staff morale. Most other companies would find themselves with no energy or motivation to continue. However, Alibaba staff retained a strong fighting spirit. They stayed in front of their computers for eight hours every day, preventing the outbreak from affecting the transactions. The entire workflow was redesigned to ensure this.

A few years later, Dai Shan, a founder member and then CFO of Alibaba, recalled: "Every day at around eight o'clock in the morning, everyone would start up their computers. They would do exactly as they were supposed to do. The only difference is that it wasn't face-to-face like before. At lunchtime they would go and make something to eat.

"They would return to their computers at about one in the afternoon. At eight or nine o'clock in the evening, they would do karaoke online together and have fun. It was all rather spontaneous, and nothing to worry about."

We can see from the above that SARS had not dissipated Alibaba's fighting spirit. On the contrary, the staff were keeping their heads held high. Perhaps this was not a co-incidence, but rather a stance that had been cultivated and accumulated over a long period of time. The 500 members of staff were scattered across the city. Strictly speaking, they had isolated and protected themselves in their homes.

The internet allowed the company leadership to give direction, and gave the staff a way to conduct their work-related tasks. Everything was clear and in good order. The company continued to run smoothly like a well-oiled machine.

Then a curious phenomenon appeared. When customers telephoned, an elderly individual would often answer with, "Hello, this is Alibaba!"

The user would be quite amazed. When did Alibaba start employing staff so advanced in years? In fact, these elderly individuals were the relatives of Alibaba staff working at home, who had warned their friends and relations that they must answer the phone in this way.

Jack Ma told his staff, "I have been extremely moved over the past few days. In response to the challenge we are facing, everyone at Ali has chosen to remain optimistic and committed. We are supporting and taking care of one another.

"Faced with the common danger of SARS, we have not forgotten the mission and responsibilities of Ali! Catastrophes will always pass eventually, and life will find a way to continue. When making a stand against disaster, we cannot cease the fight for our treasured cause!"

Of course, the dark times brought by SARS eventually dissipated. It soon became clear that Alibaba had managed to grow stronger overnight. The reason was, of course, that many businesses had started to try out the B2B market model during this difficult time.

People became aware of how convenient and fast e-commerce was when they were forced to try it. After they had tried it once, they continued to use this transaction method. From then on, Alibaba expanded with no sign of stopping.

———

It is worth mentioning another significant event that occurred during this period. The media later called it "the merging of Ya and Ba". What they were referring to was the merger and acquisition of Yahoo and Alibaba. Of course, one could also call it 'collaboration'.

Yahoo was an internet company established in the United States in 1994 by David Filo and Jerry Yang, a Chinese-American citizen. It entered the Chinese market in 1999 under the name Yahoo China.

Yahoo was one of the front-running websites in China at that time, along with Sina and Sohu. But in 2005, Jerry Yang started to feel that the operations of Yahoo China were not optimal.

Jack Ma longed to keep Alibaba running for 102 years as one of the 'top global companies'. Globalization was the only way to achieve this goal. Making an acquisition of a transnational corporation was one of the simplest yet most effective shortcuts in terms of a globalization strategy. Hence, a timely business deal was needed.

In the summer of 2005, Jack Ma received an email from Jerry Yang. The content of the email was very simple. It was an invitation for him to visit the United States and attend a Digital China Forum.

The two of them held a long discussion. They were old friends, having come into contact when Jack Ma was working at the Ministry of Foreign Trade. Jack Ma had great respect for this leading name in the online field.

Jack Ma spoke his mind freely. He expressed the need for a search engine. It was necessary for the development of any website. More and more people were starting to use search engines. If they could not find your website, then it was not worth anything.

With great foresight, Jack Ma longed to bring B2B, B2C, and C2C together, which would in turn bring China and the rest of the world together. Yet his dream could not be realized without the help of a search engine, and Yahoo's search engine was clearly first-class. So he raised the idea of collaboration with Jerry Yang, who agreed to consider it, but in a rather reserved manner. Actually, Jerry Yang was overwhelmed by Jack Ma's proposal, yet he did not give away his stance at the time.

Jerry Yang was four years younger than Jack Ma. Born in 1968 in Taiwan, he was a graduate of Stanford University in California. He was the earliest internet entrepreneur. According to Masayoshi Son, he and Jack Ma both had the same light in their eyes.

Not long after, the Beijing Wealth Forum took place. The global CEO of Yahoo, Marissa Mayer, was passing through Shanghai, and decided to pay a special visit to

Jack Ma. Mayer seemed to have come with a mission. She calmly listened to Jack Ma discuss Alibaba's global business tactics. Occasionally, she would interrupt and tell him quite clearly that collaboration with Yahoo was his best choice when it came to a global strategy.

Afterwards, Jerry Yang personally made a trip to San Francisco by car. Jack Ma met him there and they went to have a drink together and ended up continuing until midnight. Jerry Yang did not speak. Jack Ma did not have much to say either. They looked like two men drowning their sorrows together. However, they had the measure of one another and they each knew what the other was thinking.

The dim yellowish lighting and the pungent alcohol quickly brought the two men, who had originally just been friends, closer together. That evening, they were two ordinary men of flesh and blood, despite the fact that they were both huge internet tycoons. They seemed to understand each other's feelings.

A long time after, Jack Ma said during an interview with a reporter: "I felt very moved. Human sentiment worked its magic, and I realized that I had been wrong. If I did not accept, then it was possible no one else could either. Yahoo China would be faced with collapse.

"This would have a severe impact on Yahoo's global brand, and that was something I was not willing to witness, as someone who had always idolized the company. I wanted to take on the challenge, and see if I could make it work."

Perhaps human sentiment is a great enemy of businessmen in trade wars. Yet Jerry Yang gave Jack Ma an inexplicable feeling. Perhaps it was a kind of reverence or appreciation. In any case, he made the decision to go into business with Yahoo that very evening. This was not just a matter of sentiment. From a rational perspective, Jack Ma really did need the control of a company like Yahoo. Only in this manner could he turn Alibaba into a truly global internet company from the inside out.

The acquisition was formally announced on 11 August after a period of arduous negotiations. Following the announcement, Jack Ma had to begin his attempt to reform a company which was new and unfamiliar to him. This was arguably even more of a challenge, as he was practically clueless about Yahoo China.

He had not researched Yahoo China before going into talks with the central Yahoo headquarters, because Yahoo global did not want Yahoo China to find out about the move yet.

Jerry Yang and Jack Ma had always avoided mentioning Yahoo China during their discussions, so the company only became aware of its fate upon hearing the official announcement. Only then did they learn that they were already a subsidiary of Alibaba.

"I have acquired a search engine which will be the international platform and brand of the future," said Jack Ma. "I do not know any more about Yahoo than the average person, so what I have in my hands now is an unknown. However, seeing as it has over 400 employees and is a subsidiary to a multinational corporation, it is unlikely much can go wrong."

On 13 August, which was the third day following Alibaba's acquisition and partnership with Yahoo, Jack Ma and several others appeared in Yahoo China's Beijing offices. The first thing he said was, "Firstly, I am very sorry, for I was unable to communicate with you here previously due to certain regulations. Secondly, I would like to request that everyone give me an opportunity and some time. I would like to take a year to observe things here. Finally, I hope that everyone can work comfortably in the air-conditioned office."

After some investigations, he came to the conclusion that actually Yahoo China was a very Chinese company. In fact, it was more complicated than most other Chinese companies, and its performance was even more lacklustre.

He had to restructure the company and instil in it core values and a sense of direction. He needed to establish an effective system of management. He planned out a few moves. His first was to "take care of popular feeling". He said: "Many acquisitions rush straight for results from the start. Yet I believe that Alibaba is just positioning itself. It doesn't matter even if we lose a few battles."

The next move, inspired by Jack Ma's love of martial arts novels, was, "Disable power!" to use his own phrase. "Many typical companies try and increase results in the shortest amount of time possible after making an acquisition, yet in the end the results ultimately end up falling again. I think it's better to reduce productivity at the outset, and clean out all the dregs thoroughly."

However, it did not go entirely to plan.

Some of Alibaba's philosophies, such as 'passion' and 'welcoming change', were not accepted by Yahoo China, as they conflicted with its previous business culture. Yahoo China was a typical example of engineering culture. The mind won over the heart. Alibaba, on the other hand, always put passion first.

In response, Jack Ma spent several nights thinking it over: "I have acquired the company, yet it has its own ideas. As its father, it is no use for me to beat or scold it. Why not let Yahoo China establish its own working culture?

"The differences were clear from the beginning. They focus on technical staff. The north and the south of China are different. Their values are different. Their culture manifests itself differently. If this is the case, then why should the companies try and be identical?"

From then on Jack Ma gave up his power to the lower levels. He only required that, "Firstly, Yahoo gets its technology right, organizes its teams well, and forms an organization. Secondly, the company has a safe and robust structure, and improves its site traffic and revenue.

"The central goal here, and the focus of all work, should be to turn Yahoo from a high-risk into a low-risk company. Revenue is secondary."

As a result, six months, people began to find that Yahoo China was increasingly starting to follow in Alibaba's footsteps. In the past, Yahoo China's office had whitewashed walls. Now, however, they had been painted the same yellow-orange as Alibaba's. The walls were slowly covered with photographs showing off the different staff members' proudest moments. Even the bathrooms started to see some changes, with green plants and humorous posters on the walls.

At a big staff meeting six months later, Yahoo employees were no longer following a prescribed pattern when giving feedback. Each team was dressed in their own distinctive outfits. In the breaks between leaders' friendly speeches, they took turns to go up and perform on stage. Yahoo was obviously moving towards Alibaba's style of doing things.

The merging of 'Ya and Ba' gave Jack Ma a springboard which he could use to propel himself towards globalization. There was a possibility that his dream of an integrated B2B, B2C and C2C e-commerce platform would come true.

CHAPTER

7

HONOUR
AND
DEPARTURE

After the rain comes a rainbow. The philosopher Lao Tzu, who founded Taoism in the 6th century BCE, once said, "Heaven rewards the diligent." On 15 July 2000, a world-class financial magazine was published ahead of its usual schedule. More surprising still, there was a truly unforgettable figure on the front cover. His eyes were aflame, and he wore an assured smile on his face. A rather extraordinary, charming and energetic-looking Chinese man!

Forbes Magazine was founded in 1917. It is an authoritative financial magazine that has been in circulation for a whole century. It focuses on the way of thinking of the business elite, using a people-oriented philosophy and advocating the entrepreneurial spirit. It never stops at the surface level when it comes to the news. It makes an effort to clearly identify the background behind the news, and the most recent trends in business. It thoroughly investigates and researches the economics and the running of businesses.

The slogan of *Forbes Magazine* is "Never stop". It is a globally influential publication. The figure on the front cover of this particular issue was China's Jack Ma. The editors of *Forbes* had arranged a large title next to his person, "Fighting for Eyeballs", which allowed quite a lot of room for interpretation. The humorous and complimentary heading of the article inside was "Small Fry B2B".

It said in the article that Jack Ma had taken the right path. There were only 20 large companies in America whose demand was large enough to require a container's worth of hammers. Yet there were 555 wholesale hardware distributors and 20,900 retailers that only needed to purchase a small box or case of hammers. Small-scale companies like these were very grateful to Alibaba.

The experienced editor of *Forbes*, Matt Schifrin, wrote: "Although the company is registered in Hong Kong, there are thousands of businesses from over 190 countries selling all kinds of goods there.

"They have amassed 250,000 business members from all over the world since they launched in March last year. They are gaining 1,400 new registered users every day. They have over 2,000 new items listed. The growth of small fry B2B can really overtake that of a whale."

Forbes reported that they had sent their senior Asia reporter, Justin Doebele, to Shanghai and Hangzhou at the beginning of May to gather information at Alibaba for three days in order to make the front cover of this issue. In June they sent a list of 180 questions to Jack Ma to verify certain facts during their preparations. They even conducted follow-up interviews of individuals who were mentioned by Jack Ma during his interview, despite the fact that these people were located as far away as Australia and Singapore. It took them two months to meticulously produce the front cover and story.

In 2004 Jack Ma was selected as one of the top ten figures in finance for that year by China Central Television (CCTV). The CEO of Haier, a multinational consumer electronics company, presented the prize. The words he spoke before handing it over were rather brilliant: "He has wholeheartedly committed himself to matchmaking, bringing together millions of the right people. Acting as a go-between, he has connected over 200 countries and localities. By just registering your name, he can give you a whole world of choice."

In his thank-you speech, Jack Ma had this to say in response: "I would like to thank CCTV, the judges, my customers, and my colleagues. It is thanks to you all that you have made my dream become reality.

"Five years ago, at roughly this time of year, my colleagues and I spoke of our desire to create the greatest Chinese company in the world on the Great Wall. We hoped that all businessmen, wherever they were from in the world, would use our network.

"Many people thought I was a madman back then. Yet despite what people said, no one could ever change my dream to create a global company. The word mentioned most often in our company during the internet's painful years of 2001 and 2002 was 'survival'.

"Even if all other internet companies collapsed, we would keep crawling on and we would win. We forever held the belief that as long as we never gave up, our opportunity would come along. We might suffer today and tomorrow, but the day after tomorrow was going to be a good one, so no one should give up on today."

In 2005, Jack Ma was named 'Most Influential Asian Businessman' by *Forbes*.

In 2007, he was named 'Business Leader of the Year' by America's *Business Weekly*.

In March 2008, Jack Ma was named one of the Best Thirty CEOs in the World by financial magazine *Barron's*.

In July 2008, Jack Ma was presented with Japan's tenth Entrepreneur Award. In previous years, the prize had only ever been awarded to Japanese entrepreneurs.

In September 2008, Jack Ma was named one of the 'Top 25 Influential Individuals in the Internet Industry', again by *Business Weekly*. He was the only one to make it onto the list out of all the Chinese internet businesses out there. The awards he had gained on his journey were now too numerous to mention.

On 8 November 2013 he was awarded an honorary PhD in business management by Hong Kong University of Science and Technology. What did this mean for Jack Ma? It meant that he was someone who carried the air of a distinguished scholar about him, and that he was incredibly well informed.

His past awards were principally a recognition of his efforts in the business world, both in terms of leadership and influence. Without a doubt, they showed that the e-commerce model he had created was gaining recognition, and that it had made a global impact.

The confirmation by Hong Kong University of Science and Technology, with regard to his actions and his management of Alibaba, summed up the hard work he had done for this international corporation. He may never have studied business management, but he was a greatly practical man who had founded and managed a large international company. Moreover, he had maintained his vitality as the tides of time incessantly pushed his company forward. At the same time, he had transformed people's lives.

Of course, Jack Ma was fully appreciative of the degree he was awarded. After all, it was a confirmation of another side of himself. He said that before Alibaba was successful, his parents thought he would never get any higher-education qualification, and his friends feared he would never succeed. He said, charged with emotion: "My experience proves that over 80% of young Chinese people can successfully realize their dreams."

These words were heartfelt. Jack Ma had only managed to get into Hangzhou Normal University by chance, after taking the university entrance examination three times. From this perspective, he faced an insurmountable climb to reach PhD level. However, he used himself as an example to convince young Chinese people that they were all capable of getting a PhD, or becoming successful.

He also said that when he set up Alibaba before he turned 40, his wife had hoped that rather than becoming the richest man in China, he would become the most respected businessman. This was a wish that he had held on to steadfastly from beginning to end.

To an audience of graduates from Hong Kong University of Science and Technology, he said: "I hope that you all maintain a positive attitude and confidence in the future. Many people are complaining that there are no opportunities in Hong Kong any more. In reality, both Hong Kong and the mainland are full of chances. Young people need to have confidence in themselves, to never let go of hope, always persist with their dreams and never give up."

He added that Hong Kong had principally followed the Anglo-European model in the past, but now it had entered a new business model, and China was seeing some new changes too. He urged all young people to be daring enough to make a change. "Although it might be painful to do so, it will bring about less suffering than if we remain complacent with things the way they are. We must make preparations for possible rainy days ahead now, while the skies are bright and clear."

He said further that China and the world were in a state of transition, and that everyone needed to make preparations for the future, to improve and perfect themselves: "Perhaps many people think that the current transition going on now is a painful process, but actually this experience will bring about a better future for everyone."

Jack Ma had been called many names in his time, including 'King of the Internet', 'Leader of the Business World', 'Most Influential Personality', and 'Most Charismatic Personality with Future Impact'. Despite this, he remained very cautious in the face of everything. He had once been called a madman. So, after being presented with these awards, he often felt the need to come down from his ivory tower and tell people that "I am just an ordinary person. I'm a good-for-nothing really. I was born out of the times. Without the advantageous conditions I found myself in, I would be worth nothing at all. I have found success, and you can too. Actually, as long as you are hard-working, it is possible you can be even more successful than me."

The internet company Baidu gives the following explanation of what a CEO is: "The CEO system is designed to suit the modern firm. In the current market economy, the modern firm has a management structure made up of three executive components: the general shareholders, the board of directors and high-level directors. The CEO is the highest-ranking officer in the executive structure.

"The top executive officers, or top directors, are responsible to the board of directors. The board of directors gives them the authority to manage and direct company affairs. They are responsible for dealing with the daily running of the company.

"The person in charge of the executive structure is the CEO, or chief executive officer. They may be either the chairman of the board of directors, the vice-chairman or the general manager."

It is clear from the above description that the English term CEO appeared as the structure of the modern firm took shape. When Jack Ma turned his sights towards creating a company that could last for 102 years, it seemed only natural that this term would play a part in Alibaba's formation.

In truth, a CEO is different from a chairman. The CEO is one of the high-level executive officers and, of course, is the most important of them. He does not have as much power as a chairman. His role is more a case of gathering together ideas and making a final decision.

He does not just follow whatever ideas come out of his head, either. He is not an all-powerful administrator who gets the final say. You can tell from his title that it is more a case of joint discussion than arbitrary decision making. Perhaps this was just what Jack Ma had in mind in the beginning. However, when Alibaba originally set sail, first listing and then delisting from the Hong Kong stock market, it went through a great transformation from chrysalis to butterfly.

Jack Ma decided that from 10 May 2013 he would no longer act as CEO of Alibaba. He was 49 years old, and it was only his first year of being in charge of the company, yet he was going to step down from the position. He believed that the company would not be healthy if its creator could not separate himself from it.

A company could not be hijacked. A company should be run by successive generations of young, talented individuals. Just like the Yangtze River, it would flow on endlessly without any sign of ebbing. Only with a strong current would it remain steadfast and consistent. Only with a strong current would it enjoy healthy business and prospects for expansion.

On a personal level, it is also important to develop oneself and challenge one's limits. Only by continually pushing oneself can one make a leap of progress. The same is true for any company. Only with a continual supply of talent, one generation after another, can business flourish. There is nothing that always stays the same, and neither can the same person run a company forever. Everyone is always in a constant state of change. There is no way to stop this. Of course, change should be healthy and sustainable.

Naturally, the Alibaba that Jack Ma handed over was healthy. He had made substantial changes to the corporation, including the two major moves of buying back the equity shares in Yahoo and delisting from the Hong Kong Stock Exchange.

With these two moves, Alibaba became healthier and more competitive. After Lu Zhaoxi and Peng Lei were both made CEOs, experts believed that Jack Ma was capable of developing the digital platform developed by Alibaba further, and that he would take charge of the project himself. It was going to be a huge move for the expanding e-commerce industry.

While still keeping an eye on the general running of things in his role as chairman of the board, he turned his gaze to the future. This was what tactics were about – the tactics of Alibaba and of Jack Ma himself.

Many disapproved of Jack Ma's latest move, partly because it was not what they had expected. Such critics were too conservative in their attitudes to adjust to new concepts. They could not see why Jack Ma would take such a sharp turn in the opposite direction.

This instigated a lot of public discussion. There were even sensationalist headlines which appeared, such as "The Inside Story on Jack Ma's Resignation" or "The Truth About Jack Ma's Resignation."

We cannot deny the media its voice, but neither can we deny that its assessment of Jack Ma's character was rather petty. For in truth, how many 'inside stories' and 'truths' could their really be? What was really involved was his acute foresight – the resourcefulness and vision of an entrepreneur.

It was only because Alibaba was already a very healthy company that he was willing to give up his position as CEO. Jack Ma was hard-working, but not someone who was obsessed with power and money.

The year 2013 was Taobao's tenth anniversary. Jack Ma gave his 'retirement speech' to an audience of Alibaba employees, friends from all over the world, and the media:

"Today is a very special day. I have been looking forward to it for many years. Recently, I have constantly been thinking of what I should say at this gathering with all my colleagues, friends, partners, and online traders.

"However, it is rather strange. I feel like a young girl who has been looking forward to her wedding day for a long time, but now the day has arrived, does not know what to do apart from giggle. We are extremely lucky. On this day ten years ago, the SARS crisis was still raging across China. No one had any confidence.

"The young people at Ali, however, were certain that ten years on, China was going to have reached a better place, that more people would be interested in and using e-commerce. We did not expect, however, that things would have developed into the way they are today.

"I have been thinking that even if 99% of the Alibaba Corporation were to be taken away, what we have given to the company over the past decade, in terms of perseverance and our ideals, would still be worth it. I have no regrets in this life, and even less so seeing the many friends, people I trust, and people who have persevered with me.

"What has given us what we have today is also what has given me what I have today. I became successful for no reason, as did Ali. Despite this, we have kept going for many years, and are still full of hopes for the future. To tell the truth, I've been thinking this is a mater of faith.

"We chose faith when everyone else in the world had none. We chose to believe that China would be a better place in ten years to come. We chose to believe that my colleagues could do a better job than me. We chose to believe that young Chinese people could do better than we could.

"Ten or twenty years ago, I would never have thought that this would happen. I did not necessarily even believe in myself. I am particularly grateful to the faith my colleagues put in me. It is difficult to be a CEO, but even harder to be his staff.

"Now, however, people are willing to give money to a seller with the name 'Scent of a Woman' who they have never seen or heard of before, and purchase something they have never seen, which will be delivered to them from thousands of kilometres away by a stranger.

"There is trust in China now. I am so proud of all the Ali, Taobao, and Aliloan employees sitting here today. We were co-workers in this lifetime, and so shall we be in the next.

"This generation has been shown hope because of you. You are just like the post-80s and post-90s generations. You are founding a new faith which will make the world more open, transparent, sharing, and responsible. I am proud of you all.

"The world we live in today is changing. We would never have expected 30 years ago that today would be the way it is. No one would have predicted China would have become a major global manufacturer, that computers would have made such a huge impact on people's lives, or that the internet would have developed so well here. No one would have predicted that Taobao would have kept going, that Netscape would have collapsed, or that Yahoo would be the way it is today.

"The world is changing. No one would have expected that we could gather here together today and talk freely about future possibilities. Along with everyone else, I think that computers are already fast enough. Yet the internet is going to get faster. Mobile internet is here, even though many people haven't worked out what a PC network is yet. The big data age is here, even though we haven't worked out what mobile internet is yet.

"An era of change always belongs to the young people. Today, there are already many young people who have found opportunities in countless companies like Baidu, Google and Tencent [a Chinese investment holding company].

"Ten years ago, we felt utterly at a loss when faced with the countless great companies out there. Did we still have a chance? However, after ten years of perseverance and dedication, we have made it here today. If this wasn't an era of change, then the young people sitting here would not have their turn, for the industrial age of the past had a strict sense of generational hierarchy.

"We are only able to see the future now because we have taken full advantage of the changes taking place. China and the world will experience even more transformations over the next 30 years, which will give everyone a range of opportunities which we must grab firmly with both hands. Many people complain about the problems of yesterday or of 30 years ago, yet they were not alive then to experience what China and the world have gone through to get where they are too. There is no way for us to change what happened yesterday, but we can decide what the world will be like in 30 years' time. We made a change, bit by bit, by persevering for ten years. This is everyone's dream.

"I am thankful for the period of change we are going through. I am thankful for the countless people's complaints. For only when people complain do we have opportunities. Only when there is change can we be clear what we have, what we want, and what we should give up.

"It has been an honour for me to be a part of the 14-year journey it has taken to establish Alibaba. I am a businessman, and now humanity has entered an e-commerce economy. What is regretful, however, is that businessmen have still not gained the respect they deserve. Businessmen are no longer solely focused on making profit.

"Just like any other profession, including art, education, and politics, we too are doing our best to make this a better world to live in.

"Being a businessman for nearly 14 years has made me understand what life, hardship, perseverance, and responsibility are, and how to tell the difference between one's own success and that of others'. What we look forward to is seeing our staff smile.

"After midnight tonight, I will no longer be CEO. Starting from tomorrow, business will just be my hobby.

I am deeply proud of my 14 years in business. Seeing you here, seeing young people in China, I hope that our golden years will not be wasted. No one in the world can predict how long you will be successful for. No one can say whether or not you will fail, age, or mentally deteriorate. The only way to prevent yourself from failure, ageing, and mental deterioration is to believe in young people, for young people are our future.

"Therefore, I will not return to Alibaba as CEO again. I will not come back even if I want to, because there would be no use in me doing so. You will do it better. I am proud of how much the company has expanded, but I know it has only just started in terms of its contribution to society. Hence, everyone at Ali is very excited, diligent, and hard-working. Through all this, though, we are all just ordinary people who live earnestly and take pleasure in our work. What we have gained has already far exceeded what we put in. Current society is pushing for us to keep going for a long time, for we can solve social problems. There are so many problems to be solved in society today, and there are opportunities for all of us. Without these problems, we would not be here.

"Everyone at Ali has persevered in providing services for small businesses, for they are where the Chinese dream can be found to be most flourishing. Fourteen years ago, we promised to 'make doing business easy for everyone'. Now, the task of helping small businesses grow is on your shoulders. There is something else I want to say on the topic of small businesses. Someone once said that the internet has resulted in inequality. In my opinion, however, what the internet has really created is equality. Just think, in which province, city, or locality are there favourable taxation laws for small businesses and start-ups? Only on the internet. There, small businesses can gain up to five or six million users in just three to five years. After they have expanded, they still demand the same advantages. Small businesses just need a discount of 500 yuan on their tax rates. If everyone at Ali supports them, then they will most certainly become some of the biggest taxpayers in China of the future.

"I would like to express my gratitude to everyone. From now on, I will undertake a few projects that interest me, like education and environmental protection. There was that song which just came out, *Heal the World*, but actually there are many problems in this world that we cannot resolve. There is only one Obama, yet too many people see themselves as being like him. Actually, it is enough for us to do one job that we are interested in well. We must put in hard work, not just in the workplace, but to improve China's environment, to ensure water runs clear, the sky is blue, and food is safe. I plead for everyone to do this.

"I am very honoured to introduce the future Ali team. They have worked alongside me for many years, so that now they understand me better than I do myself. Lu Zhaoxi has 13 years of experience. He has held many positions in Alibaba and experienced many trials and tribulations. What I should say is, there has been a comparable amount of tears and laughter over the past 13 years. It is very difficult to take on the role of Jack Ma.

The reason I am standing here today is because everyone believed in me. It was simple because of their faith.

"I implore those who supported me to support the new team and Lu Zhaoxi in the same way, to believe in the new team and Lu Zhaoxi in the same way. Thank you all. From tomorrow onwards, I will have a new life. I am lucky that I am able to retire at the age of just 48. Work was my life before now. From tomorrow, life will be my work. Let us welcome Lu Zhaoxi."

APPENDIX

TRANSCRIPT OF
JACK MA'S SPEECH
AT THE ZHEJIANG
ENTREPRENEURS'
ASSOCIATION
IN 2016

ENTREPRENEURS ARE
WILD ANIMALS

I think Zhejiang's entrepreneurs are pretty incredible. It's hard to train someone to become an entrepreneur. They are more likely to be discovered. I've said before that I am opposed to my company being run by professional managers. That's the reason why I designed a partner mechanism seven years ago.

What's the difference between an entrepreneur and a professional manager? The example I used back then to get everyone on board was to imagine that both an entrepreneur and a professional manager were hunting wild boar on a mountain. The difference is, if a professional manager fires a shot at a wild boar and misses, and the boar charges at him, then he will fling his gun to one side and run away. Yet if an entrepreneur like us fires a shot at a wild boar and misses, and the boar charges at him, then he will take any knife or stick that he has on his person and charge right back at it. The entrepreneur is not afraid of anything. We were not trained to be the way we are – we are a product of market conditions. I still think that there are not many good economists out there, are there?

There certainly are some very good economists, but can anyone here tell me of someone whose start-up succeeded after listening to the advice of an economist? Sometimes, people even end up failing after taking their advice. You originally knew what you wanted, but after hearing the economist say that this aspect of the economy is going to deteriorate, or that this is a troubling situation, you don't know what to do any more.

You don't know what to do apart from panic. You don't know what to do about what he is concerned about. You don't know where to start with the things he said would help.

GOOD NEWS
AND BAD NEWS

"The ducks are the first ones to sense that the spring river water is warming up."[5] We entrepreneurs have our own sense of intuition. What we need is to keep calm and conduct a rational and perceptive analysis of things. The economy is just like playing mah-jong. If you have some bad luck, then just have a break, walk around, and have some tea before coming back to the game table. It is very rare to find a group of entrepreneurs as hard-working as this one here in Zhejiang. Even though it is only the beginning of the new year, everyone has already sat down and started to work out some strategies.

There are many people here. This makes me think, if Zhejiang entrepreneurs cannot find a way to survive, or if there is something they cannot resolve, then neither will any other group of entrepreneurs in China be able to solve it.

I said last time that working out one's principles is very important. Today, I'm going start by telling everyone a piece of bad news. The outlook for the economic situation this year is not good, and it might remain that way for a long time.

At the same time, I am going to tell everyone a piece of good news. Everyone is in a bad situation together. No

[2] From the poem *Evening Scene at the Spring River* by the Song Dynasty poet Su Shi.

one has it good, so this is a piece of good news, because if there were people who it was going well for, and not for you, then it's you who are unfortunate. If everyone is in a bad situation together, then it's actually better. So there is nothing to be worried about. Sometimes, it has nothing to do with you personally whether the economic situation is good or not. There are still a lot of awful enterprises to be found when the economy is doing well, and many great ones when it is in trouble. Not many of China's best enterprises were born during times of prosperity. I am particularly interested in instances where enterprises have failed, because I don't know much about technology, management, or finance. If we look at the process of an enterprise's development, and which difficulties it must go through, then you will find that in times of economic difficulty, 80 to 90% of good enterprises will experience three to four particularly challenging periods.

If an enterprise has not experienced a challenging period, internal trouble or external battles, then there is no way it can weather stormy seas.

Please don't call yourself an investor if you make money when the stock market is looking healthy. You can only truly be called an investor if you make a profit when the stock markets are in trouble. I cannot understand why people would call themselves investors during a time when any old lady on the street could make money from buying some stocks. I don't really like this kind of behaviour. So, why do I say that the economic situation now is not good?

There seems to be a series of factors involved. The USA's raised interest rates, the outflow of capital, the depreciation of Renminbi,[6] the fluctuation of the stock market, the decrease in exports, the weak growth of the import sector, production surplus, the depression of the real economy, the large slump in commodity prices, entrepreneurs' lack of faith, the slowdown or development of emerging economies, the environment reaching its limits for capacity, and the worsening of air pollution. Well, in any case, there is no one who would say they are having an easy time. The real economy complains of the internet. The internet blames the real economy. The government says enterprises are not doing things right. Enterprises say that the government is not doing things right. In any case, it seems that it is not a good situation. However, everyone must remember that no reform has ever occurred during times of peace and prosperity. Reform occurs out of necessity. Innovation also occurs out of necessity. Seeing how bad things are at the moment, it seems reform is inevitable.

---

[3] *Renminbi* is the official name of the currency introduced by the Communist People's Republic of China at the time of its foundation in 1949. It means 'the people's currency'.

A STORM IS COMING
– IT'S BETTER TO HIDE THAN BRAVE THE RAIN

I often remind myself of a story. A storm is on its way. There are three people. One has a very good umbrella, one has a very good raincoat, and one has neither. When the storm finally arrives, the two people with an umbrella and a raincoat go out, assuming they will be able to reach their destination. In the end, neither of them do, for one of them slips and breaks their leg and one of them slips and breaks their back. The person without a raincoat or umbrella, however, spent just two hours of his time waiting inside, loosening up his limbs. When the rain stops he runs out the door, and is actually still the first one to reach his destination. Therefore, when the economy is looking gloomy, I implore everyone to remain calm and objective. We need to be rational and perceptive. I hope that everyone notes that it is easy to understand what I am saying, but quite difficult to put it into practice.

Economists and academics always talk in a very complicated-sounding manner, yet they do not necessarily understand when it comes to putting things into practice. We entrepreneurs, on the other hand, might not be able to out-talk others, but we know what we have to do. Let us talk about China's GDP. Before the reform and opening-up period, China's GDP was about as high as that of the poorest country in Africa.

Before the reform of state-owned enterprises, they were making a loss of up to 85%. Before the reform of the financial system, China's four main banks were principally engaged in assets. Now, however, some of the biggest global banks are Chinese. The reforms which took place were concerned with production. There was a serious excess in production. It had to be reformed. China was producing 100,000 tons of steel. It only needed 60,000, making an excess of almost 50%.

There was a great pressure on the entire nation. Let me tell you all, the economic situation is not looking good. You say the internet is not a good thing, that we are walking on thin ice. Go and examine real enterprises. The banks have survived for over 40 years. There are several internet companies that have survived for over a decade. Which ones have been active for over five years?

Everyone is talking about innovation, but no company can afford to keep on innovating constantly. We paid 17 billion yuan in taxes in Zhejiang Province last year. What are we going to do next year?

If we keep on going on like this, then a day will certainly come when we collapse. There has to be a day when we stop innovating. How can we keep it going? How can we keep reforming the culture of our organization?

Just like the weather, you already know a bad spell has arrived. When you are sure of the conditions, then what is most important is to decide what action you will take, and not wait for the sun to come out. I tell you all, there is no use in waiting for a change in circumstances.

Looking at the next 5 to 15 months, I believe that the slowdown of the economy will continue for quite a time. It's not going to be temporary. It doesn't matter whether we maintain 7% growth or not. One of the key indicators of performance our company has used over the past few years is quite different to everyone else's. Some of our departments do measure performance by growth, yet there are also some which are rewarded if they are able to undertake a task this year with 3,000 people that they required 5,000 people to complete the last. Sometimes, growth is not as important as making job cuts. There are also certain areas which can be got rid of, and shutting these areas down is worthy of reward. Today, therefore, we must consider the internal workings of our companies. We must be clear on which areas can be got rid of, which methods must be changed, which departments can be shut down, which *must* be shut down. We have to do this now, because there are some operations which cannot be stopped. However, I am optimistic about the Chinese economy for the next 5 to 15 years. Why am I optimistic? Actually it has a lot to do with the reforms and policy making going on right now. The anti-corruption movement has laid a foundation for the market economy to become more transparent and standardized. However, reducing corruption is in itself a very painful process.

Secondly, poverty reduction is a huge opportunity. China has done two things that no one has dared to do in the past thousand years. No one has taken on corruption with so much force. They said that they would wipe out poverty. There is no nation or era in the past thousand years that has dared to make these proposals. I think that the Communist Party is very admirable for actually having done so. There is nothing which cannot be done if you put your mind to it. Seeing as they have decided to do it, then it must be done properly. This is a huge opportunity.

Thirdly, I believe that the government's influence over the economy will continue to weaken over the next 5 to 15 years. What does that signify?

It means that both the market and enterprises in general will become increasingly stronger. We just have to remember this point, everybody. In the past, we relied on policies. Of course some people mentioned land resources. In the past, we relied on licences. It wasn't seen as a skill for people to rely on selling land or mineral resources. From now on, we will rely on the value created from land, policies, licences, raw materials, and minerals. As long as your company can create value and maintain it, then you have a chance at surviving in the market economy.

GOVERNANCE IS AS PAINFUL AS HAVING A TOOTH EXTRACTED

Many enterprises today are suffering. Let me tell you all what will happen if you don't change the sources of suffering.

As we move further towards a market-based economy, the first source of suffering is the global economic downturn.

There is a second source of suffering. In the past decade, your organizational structure, company culture, and business model might have done well, but as we move further towards a market mechanism in the next 5 to 15 years, you will die a hard death if your structure, culture, staff, and organization are not suited to the changes.

Let me share with you all some information about our company. What our company has been most concerned about internally in the past three to five years, especially in the past three to five months, is what kind of organization, staff, and culture is suited to the developments coming in the next 5 to 15 years. Of course, transformation comes at a cost. Just like having a tooth out, it's going to hurt. If you don't have it pulled out, however, then it will continue to ache every single day. You won't die, but you will feel like you're hovering between life and death. I hope that everyone is going to make adequate preparations. We must mentally prepare ourselves to endure the labour pains of reform. We must fight through it. Some things are already decided. The value of staple commodities is going to drop. Outdated enterprises are going to be shut down and transferred. Things which could be sold in the past might not be able to be sold any more. Let me tell you all, this pressure is real. Don't start talking about what the real economy is doing. According to the internet economy, the rankings of Baidu, Alibaba, and Tencent are going to decrease very rapidly. We are still unsure of who is going to come along and take over from us. We worry every day about how long we can last.

SELF-TURMOIL, THE TURMOIL OF A CEO

No enterprise can withstand a long-term ordeal. If you want to, you must put yourself through a constant state of turmoil. Don't blame the market. It's better to take a good hard look at yourself. Crisis is coming. Actually, in times of crisis, it is not company staff who should be reassessed.

Rather, there are two other things we should reassess. The first is the CEO, and the second is the company itself – whether its original culture can withstand the times. How should we assess the CEO? What is a CEO?

Everyone knows that a CEO is principally in charge of two tasks. When times are good, the CEO must make decisions about which things are not worthwhile and must be got rid of. They are disasters waiting to happen if they are not eliminated. In times of difficulty, the CEO must find where opportunities lie. When your staff have full confidence in the CEO, he must be careful, and when they are showing signs of grievances he must seek out opportunities. This is the CEO, this is a leader, they have ultimate responsibility. Only a leader can carry out this kind of duty. A professional manager does not think much about problems like these. The mark of a true CEO is foresight, open-mindedness, and strength.

What does foresight mean? Foresight is the perspective, depth, and breadth with which you look at a problem. Hence, some people say, "Jack Ma, you are a gifted speaker." Actually, I have never thought I was a very good speaker. It seems I've never used many things like adjectives in my speeches. I really don't think I am particularly eloquent, but I do think that the perspective, depth, and breadth with which I look at problems is different to other people. I hope everyone realizes this.

You look at problems from the perspective of your company and your industry, especially in times like these. I hope that now general conditions are looking bad, there is an economic downturn, and your companies are faced with difficulty, that all the bosses out there can keep calm and answer the following questions: "What kind of company did you want to set up in the beginning? Are the things you wanted in the beginning still here today? What do you want now? What do you believe in?"

What I am referring to is not what other people are saying about which industry is doing well, what those competitors are doing, or what the government is supporting. What I am referring to is whether or not you are clear on whether this is what you want to do, that you will do it or die trying. Think of a clear answer to these questions, for you only have a chance if you can do so, and if you are doing what you are passionate about and what you believe in, and then bring together the people who believe in you and what you are doing.

The second important factor is open-mindedness. During the course of reform, young people have become a significant force in society. Young people have quite different ideas to you, so let me ask you all to pay attention and listen carefully. Actually, young people are not always right, but a lot of things they say are different to us, and this is important for broadening your mind.

The third thing is resilience. Please don't go about with blind optimism or pessimism. At the end of every year for the past ten years, I have always taken a look at the next 12 months. My company staff are already used to me doing this. It got quite difficult to make any predictions for 2004 after the year 2003, and 2005 was extremely difficult. To be honest, the right thing to do is to remain calm and optimistic when you meet with a challenge. Yet if you do not notice what challenges you are going to face in the future, then you are just being blindly optimistic. As an entrepreneur or someone who does business, you must be clear on what has the power to threaten you in your industry. You don't necessarily have to be clear on what has the power to make you thrive, but you must be clear on what might threaten you. I have met many entrepreneurs who have talked about big opportunities which are simply just going to be a success. It seems there is no one who has ever chatted to me about which aspects their company is *not* doing well on. The future has the power to swallow people up, even if they are often very impressive, often because of luck. What is luck?

Luck is something we cannot be certain of. Many people focus on external factors, and very few look internally. Very few people question themselves. The difference between Alibaba and other people is that we spend the most time thinking about how to adapt ourselves to the future.

DON'T TAKE SLEEPING PILLS DURING THE DAYTIME

Let me give you all an example. In 2012, when the economy was looking its best, our company created an internal budget for 2013. In the budget, we doubled our predicted targets, profits, and income. Alibaba was doing rather awesomely in 2012. Taobao and [its B2C spin-off] Tmall were wildly successful. I said that we had to double our current figures, but really I knew that even if I hadn't said so, we would have doubled them anyway. What were the demands we had to meet to double our figures, though?

Please could everyone draw up a budget for me which outlines how many staff I would need to hire to double the company figures? At that time, we had a total of 20,000 employees. According to the budget we drew up that year, we would need another 8,700 to double all our targets. I said no, and that I would not accept such an increase.

The second budget drawn up said that 7,800 people were required, but I would not accept that figure either. In the last meeting, they asked me how many people would I actually accept? I said, "What do you think?" They said an extra 5,000 people. I said no. They said "Then how many people do you think?"

I said 200 people. Any more that 200 people, and none of the staff, including the management and myself, would get any bonuses. I said that: "Every year people tell me to increase my personnel, but I do not want to. Just double our figures for me, and keep the staff increase within 200 people."

What happened in the end?

We reached double of all our targets, and there was a net reduction of 300 members of staff. Reform was forced into happening!

The people below me told me, very strangely, that we must increase our number of staff and budget by a certain amount to achieve our goals. I said that we had to do it this way, that there was no budget and that we couldn't increase the number of people, but we still had to think of a way. I racked my brains alongside everyone else. According to our previous and current assessments, when Taobao was established, hiring one new employee cost 100 million yuan's worth of sales. That includes the associated increase in cleaners and security guards for the building. I am against hiring more staff because each one means an extra 100 million. If you take away the option of increasing staff, then the group of people already there will be forced to think of a way to innovate their technology, products, and organization. If you don't, then they will just mess things up by forever increasing staff, raw materials, and other things.

So, when things are going well, people need to apply some pressure. The stock market's circuit breaker is not a bad thing; it was just launched at the wrong time. China's stock market is already very fragile. There was nothing wrong with taking a sleeping pill for its problems, but now it's taken it, it seems unable to wake up because it's very unhealthy. Even the best creations still need the right time to make them happen. We say we need to do the right thing at the right time, so there are still great future opportunities.

CONSUMER-DRIVEN

Why do American heroes never die? Firstly, I think everyone should remember that the driving force of consumerism is like a wind tunnel. It's incredibly powerful. China's consumer market is currently situated in a completely unique position. It is very rare to see such a large consumer wind tunnel, so I hope that everyone will re-examine the Chinese consumer market. You only have a chance at establishing yourself here if you understand the Chinese market and its rules. You have to understand the market itself before you can understand its rules. Sometimes everyone thinks that, everyone seems to be copying the USA now. Sometimes things that worked very well in the USA are ineffective in China. Why is that?

It is because the USA spends other people's money and the money of tomorrow. We Chinese people, however, spend our own money, and the money of yesterday. The two markets have totally different personalities. American people are rational when it comes to making investments and perceptive when it comes to spending money. Chinese people, everyone sitting here and myself included, are very rational when it comes to spending money and perceptive when it comes to making investments.

We are very impulsive when buying stocks, but ever so tight-fisted when buying even the smallest of things. People might scrimp and save for an entire year just to blow it all on stocks, for stocks are something everyone is very interested in, but we think it will mess everything up if we spend money on adding new equipment or staff.

I have spoken about morale and staff pay rises before. Please remember that morale is to be found in the ranks of the foot soldiers. I have noticed that many companies, especially international ones, give their senior management pay rises. Chinese companies, however, need to give their ordinary staff pay rises. This needs to happen. There is no real difference if you pay senior management 50,000 or 10,000 yuan a month. He just thinks, "Well, I already have 2 million, right?"

However, if you raise the wages of your ordinary staff by 5,000 or 3,000 yuan, then they will be extremely grateful. Morale is to be found in the ranks of the foot soldiers. So, as you can see, many things are different. Even the way we play sports is different. Everyone else plays sports with big balls, but we use small ones.[4] With everyone else's ball games, you have to be brave enough to go on the offensive. For us, however, it is better to stick to the rules. When playing the business game, US companies are always on the offensive, but before they go for a collision, they set up a lot of game rules. China does not like to make collisions, because our game rules are quite disordered. Even our movies are different. All the heroes in American movies survive in the end, while heroes in Chinese films end up dying. For us, you are only a hero

---

[4] Jack Ma is comparing ping-pong, favoured in China, and games like basketball and football which are favoured by other countries.

if you die, so who is left to be a hero afterwards? After watching some Chinese movies, you will find that basically all the heroes die. If all the heroes die, then who is left to be one? American heroes are always baddies until it comes to a crucial moment when they have to become goodies. Shortly after, they become bad again, because they are just ordinary people.

Therefore, I hope everyone remembers that there are still American people who don't understand China, while Chinese people spend all their time researching the US. We need to spend time researching ourselves, our unique market and its rules. We need to research what's going on beneath the new state of the economy and the new normal. Actually, we think that we need to understand human nature, the market, and the state of Chinese society.

USING MOVIES TO UNDERSTAND CONSUMERISM AND NEW ENTITIES

The USA has already progressed from an investment to a consumer economy. Before Ronald Reagan became president, the economy of the USA was also driven by investments and exports. Later on, it became consumer-driven. I hope that we too can learn how to be consumers. Last night, I watched two movies. How many people here watch at least one movie every month? How many people haven't watched a movie for more than six months?

Not bad. I think some people are too embarrassed to put their hands up. Actually, there is a problem that I noticed about three to five years ago. I noticed that I did not understand what many young people in our company were talking about. They laughed, but I did not know what they were laughing about. I didn't understand what the words they were using meant. Afterwards, I found out that I didn't understand the popular sayings that they were using from TV shows and movies at all. New things often now appear on TV shows and movies first. Therefore, it is not enough to get a few clients together and have a discussion if you want to understand the market. Rather, it is going online and finding out what young people need.

Young people are definitely the key for finding new openings in the consumer market. Looking at young people is looking at the future. Now, there are 2 billion young people born during or after the 1980s. This is the largest number ever seen in history. There are people complaining about the internet economy, but I tell you all, do not complain. It will still exist if you complain about it or not, and it's growing faster and faster. On Singles Day[5] this year, everyone was saying that the real economy was not doing well. Let me tell you all, on Singles Day this year, 75% of sellers were new entities. These companies had never been heard of three years ago. China has given birth to an array of new entities, which are a response to consumer' needs, especially emerging communities, new young people and new consumers. They were unheard of before new needs emerged. Therefore, new entities and new consumerism are in the process of being born. It is not that entities are failing, it is *your* entities that are failing. It is not sales which are failing, it is the sales of *your* companies which are failing.

People say that their sales have taken a hit from the internet industry. Let me tell you all, 20 years ago, you took down state-owned department stores and street vendors. Back then, you were the ones leading, creating, and developing demand. Twenty years later, and you have not maintained your client relationships well, and are not providing good customer service. As a result, things are now orienting towards the internet, which understands customer' demands better. They have taken you out. This is only to be expected.

[5] A festival celebrated on 11 November by young, single people in China.

DON'T MISS OUT ON THE POWERFUL WIND TUNNELS OF REFORM, SCIENCE, AND TECHNOLOGY

The second wind tunnel with driving force is that of reform. It is once in a blue moon that China finds itself in a period of reform like the current one. I think that there are already many reforms underway, especially those aimed at anti-corruption. The reforms aimed at anti-corruption and eliminating poverty are opportunities never seen before in the past 1,000 years. You might have heard it before, but I want to tell everyone once more, that these are two great chances that we must not overlook. For 800 of the past 1,000 years, China's GDP outstripped that of any other nation on the planet. However, in the most recent two centuries, it fell behind. Thanks to the reform and opening up, it managed to move back up to second place. Actually, I think that the reform and opening up, especially today when the economy is in such dire straits, I think that it is very rare for reform to be forced out of market pressures. However, we should not wait for reform to arrive, but create it ourselves. Stimulating reform starts with reforming your own company. If you take action yourself, then you don't have to spend time waiting. I have discovered recently that there is something rather strange going on with Chinese companies. Everyone is complaining about the government, but no one ever says what they have not being doing well in the past two or three years. When we are successful, we always say how awesome we are, but when we fail we just blame the government and the market. This is quite embarrassing. Does the government have anything to do with whether you succeed or not? Yes, but so do your personal decisions, your team, company culture, and charisma. Hence, I hope that everyone can make the most of the great wind tunnel that reforms are bringing.

Thirdly, it's the wind tunnel brought about by science and technology. Internet companies have done very well during the past 20 years. Yet you can't really tell anything from just 20 years. Every time there is a revolution in science and technology, the first 20 years are spent on building up the technology; it is only in the following 30 years that the technology is truly applied. This was clearly the pattern seen in the 50 years it took for steam engines to take off for the engineering industry.

When it came to the second technological revolution, it also took approximately 50 years for the whole of America's energy sector to completely revolutionize. The first 20 years were spent on the technology, and the following 30 on its application. It is only in the final 30 years that any technological revolution finally comes into effect. Therefore, what I want to tell you all today is that the internet companies that have been in existence for 20 years now, or 21 years now, will inevitably go through the same process in the next 30 years. The transformations which have already occurred have far exceeded everyone's expectations. In my view, we were not ready. Everyone talks too much and takes too little action. So, I hope that you all pay attention to the fact that in the next 20 to

30 years, there will be an innumerable succession of new companies that will come onto the scene, and even more companies that will fail.

It was like this for the 20 to 30 years of the first and second technological revolutions. In the next ten years of this one, what is going to happen will far exceed what we are expecting, I tell you all, including the transformations and attacks on our organizations. During the first technological revolution, the business model that was born out of the industrial revolution was the factory.

The business model brought about by the second, energy-related, revolution was the firm. What business model will be born in the next 30 years? Has anyone thought about this?

Right now, the reforms you are instigating in your small organizations and fast-paced culture are crossing boundaries. Let me tell you all, organizational structure is going through a significant period of reform now. I hope everyone will attach adequate importance to this fact, which I will talk about in more detail shortly. The good news is, Chinese enterprises don't have to be too concerned, because most of us Zhejiang businesses have only been around for 10 to 15 years. It is incredibly painful for companies that have been around for something like 80 or even 100 years. Now, you still have a chance, because you have only been around for about a decade and only have 2,000 to 3,000 members of staff. If you had over 10,000 members of staff, undertaking any reform would be so excruciatingly painful that your whole operation might go to pieces.

The penetration of mobile phone ownership in farming, low-income and uneducated households has now reached 90%. In the past, it was only high-income households which reached this figure. Now, low-income households have reached it too. This is a transformation that no one expected to see. The amount of data and information that has precipitated in the past few decades since the human race entered the internet era is already greater than that which was amassed over the past 2,000 years using print and other ways of sharing information. I would like to share with you all the significance of this fact. The first, industrial revolution set mankind free, and replaced workers with machinery. During the second technological revolution, sustained development of energy resources allowed mankind to reach the moon. Further and further we went. However you look at it, the previous two revolutions were physical transformations. This revolution is much more frightening, for it is a mental transformation of our minds and thoughts. It is the continual transformation of the human mind. It will change our intelligence. Therefore, in the future, I hope that everyone will pay attention to the fact that the most important transformation going on outside of new energy development is in biotechnology, and it's increasing in speed, especially with cloud computing and large data. Humanity's health requirements are increasing. The demands on companies have increased since the third technological revolution.

CUSTOMERS FIRST, SHAREHOLDERS THIRD

All enterprises have entered the data-technology era. All enterprises are transparent and engage in sharing. All enterprises must innovate and find a way to be unique, to stand out from the crowd. Why is this?

It's because consumers are demanding greater transparency and a greater level of information sharing. Consumers will inevitably require you to offer new things. They like things they can't find anywhere else, that no one else has. If you are not consumer-driven, then you will not survive. I said during my speech at Wall Street in New York in 2007, our company is different to others. We put our customers first, staff second, and shareholders third. The people at Wall Street pretty much fainted when they heard this. They said that all companies put shareholders first. I think that shareholders are important, but out of the three, it is customers who make you profit and staff who create value. If customers create profit and staff create value, then shareholders are naturally very pleased. Consequently, everything must revolve around our clients and consumers. This kind of company only has a chance of survival in the 21st century. The so-called revolution is changing yourself to adapt to consumers and other demands. If this doesn't form part of your thinking, then your plight will just become more and more tragic.

RESEARCH AUTOMOBILES, NOT HORSE DUNG

The world of the future will not be built on economies of scale. Many economic theories are undergoing great change. In the future, economics will not be based on economies of scale, on money, power, or influence. It will be built on knowledge, intelligence, and innovation. Actually, there are many problems that are not worth us worrying about, for they will disappear by themselves during the course of development. In the past, when people travelled around on horseback, there was a lot of filthy horse dung on the roads. People would try and avoid it. How was the problem resolved?

Some people swept it up, while others flattened it. In the end, it was the arrival of the automobile that brought about the end of horse dung. While everyone else was focused on what to do with the dung, there were some people who had turned their attention to researching automobiles. The people who are going to succeed are those who understand the future. Quite often, your company has this problem and that problem which needs resolving. What do you think it means to take a one-time look at the future?

I hope everyone will spend more time on examining things. Everything requires forward thinking. Changing only feels meaningful when it's for the future. Professional managers went through a lot of plans for the past. Most of these looked at which plans should be used to solve the companies' current problems. This is an ineffective method. Real tactics should look at: Where will our customers be in the future? Where will our partners head for? Which wind tunnels do we have to secure to make sure they stay with us?

KEEP RISKS OUTSIDE THE SCENE OF THE FIRE

The first method I came up with seven or eight years ago when I was researching different strategies was: "When you come across a forest fire, should you run at it head on and try to put it out?"

When I had just started out back then, it was the fires that broke out on the Daxing'anling mountain range [in 1987] that led me to consider this question. Should the firefighters attack the fire head on? Or cut down all the trees 50 kilometres [30 miles] around it and dig a moat? The wind would stop there. The sacrifice you made by cutting down the trees would prevent further loss. Otherwise, if you keep fighting it head on more and more people will die in the process. Currently, many companies are too busy thinking about how to solve the problems of the past or the present that they forget to think about how to solve the problems of the future. What will your customers be like in the future? What will your consumers, company and staff be like? I hope that everyone will think about these questions with some foresight.

So, when running a business, you must consider what your original intentions were, what you already have, what you want, and what you have to let go of.

When a business reaches a certain scale, it has to learn how to let go. It's not that you are doing badly; everyone is. Panic will just make everyone more confused. By all means, do not make any wrong moves or blunders during times of chaos. Do not make any rash decisions during times of difficulty. Often, difficulties are not caused by other people, but by yourself. Among the Zhejiang entrepreneurs sitting here, no one has got so big that they can turn the economic situation bad, or make things go bad for me. The large proportion of entrepreneurs sitting here do not have that kind of influence. If your business has reached quite a large scale, and the economic situation is that you are doing worse and worse, you can only blame yourself for not seeing it coming over the past few years. You are responsible for the disaster. I hope that everyone can remain equal during adverse conditions. In the past, people paid attention to building a network of connections. Now, they are focused on building insight and foresight. In the past, people relied heavily on licences. Now, they rely on ability. Hence, have a think about what entrepreneurship really means.

What does perseverance mean today? How did you get where you are today? What will you be doing tomorrow? I also hope that people stop making summaries of where the government is going wrong in its supervision. We should be making a summary of what we have personally done wrong and what we still have not changed, even though we have regretted it for a long time.

YOUR DOCUMENTS CAN'T BE TOO LONG, AND YOU CAN'T MAKE LARGE-SCALE STAFF CUTS

I have a few things to say about the documents published from a few recent national conferences. They seem to be getting longer and longer. It's like when you are communicating with your staff. You have to be absolutely clear on which A, B, and C you need to change. You cannot start saying, "I don't want this and that changed, I don't want that thrown out, this can be kept, but that can't." You'll be left in a complete mess.

In the same way, some of those documents are so long that you end up feeling quite muddled after reading them. Somewhere along the way, reading about 'Agriculture is the foundation', 'Science and technology are the future', 'Industry is progress', 'Education is the key', you end up not even knowing where to start. Actually, there are only a few items which are important, and they can be condensed down into the three things that must be done in 2016. Everything else, you can do what you personally see fit. This makes the goals very clear.

The government has to take care of everything when making policies. That's the difference between us and them. When it comes to remodelling a company, you must state which things need to be changed and which things need to be thrown out, and clearly. Do not make staff cuts lightly before a time of crisis. Sometimes, there are great repercussions that follow staff cuts. When making cuts, please remember that it is a last resort. It is like undergoing a serious surgical operation. By all means, do not cut staff as a preventative measure before the operation. Take care when recruiting.

Sometimes, it is necessary to have an operation. Just please do not make staff cuts. What I mean is, problematic staff should, of course, got rid of, but large-scale cuts are extremely harmful.

Of course, I hope everyone does not forget to remain calm when faced with difficulty. It is easier said than done to remain calm. So, when the market rescue worth 4 trillion happened, it was my view that the businesses that were going to go under should not be saved. Taxes should be collected as normal during difficult periods. There will still be growth and businesses with prospects. They are where resources should be spent.

This is relevant to everyone here. Take a look at which of your departments are doing well, and increase the supply of resources to the successful areas. Examine which areas are not doing so well, and shut down the ones which need to be.

You see, I'm involved in football, and once someone asked me why I invested in Evergrande. Evergrande was the only football club doing well in China two years ago. When a fire dies, everyone disappears along with it. When a fire starts, people amass there. Similarly, resources should be concentrated in the company's best departments and the industries of tomorrow. Those that need to be shut down should be. For sometimes you have spoken about doing it for a long time but cannot bring yourself to do it. "The ducks are the first ones to sense that the spring river water is warming up." Every company has its own problems. However, it also has its own strengths. A company's pain points are not necessarily a bad thing. If you manage to surmount them then it can actually make you stronger. However, you must ask yourself what price you are willing to pay to do so.

LEARN FROM THE
CULTIVATION OF NANNIWAN

There is a final point I would like to mention with regard to enterprises in the 21st century. I just talked about transforming organizational structure, and this deserves our attention. In adverse economic conditions, organization, personnel, and company culture all need to be strengthened from the inside. Does everybody know what Mao Zedong did?

When Mao Zedong reached Yan'an [in Shaanxi Province] with the Communist Party [during the Long March of 1934–1935], the Red Army had already run out of steam. You might say the situation was pretty bad. Where had their good luck gone? Anyway, they were in Yan'an. Mao Zedong was responsible for three quite extraordinary feats. At the Chinese Anti-Japanese Military and Political University he trained his cadres. During the Rectification Movement at Yan'an he united people's values, sense of mission, and remoulded their ideals. Thirdly, he cultivated the land left barren in Nanniwan [gorge, to the southeast of Yan'an]. In adverse economic conditions, all enterprises should consider a set of questions and maintain a sense of idealism and positivity about the future. You should be clear on what your company does well that other people do not, and rely on this. Following this comes the retraining of your 'cadres' or staff. In good times, everyone relies on the market for their operations, but in bad times we should remain calm and learn more about management, reorganization and remodelling our personnel. Send the bad ones out and bring good ones in. People who are still willing to join your company when you're going through a bad time are often quite clear about what they want. The lesson we can learn from the cultivation of Nanniwan is that in times of difficulty, we should all guard the land we have and focus on producing good output figures.